William Stephen, pseud. Old Indian

Historical Sketch of Armenia

and the Armenians in ancient and modern times

William Stephen, pseud. Old Indian

Historical Sketch of Armenia
and the Armenians in ancient and modern times

ISBN/EAN: 9783337288280

Printed in Europe, USA, Canada, Australia, Japan

Cover: Foto ©Andreas Hilbeck / pixelio.de

More available books at **www.hansebooks.com**

HISTORICAL SKETCH

OF

Armenia and the Armenians

IN ANCIENT AND MODERN TIMES,

WITH

SPECIAL REFERENCE TO THE PRESENT CRISIS.

BY

AN OLD INDIAN.

LONDON:
ELLIOT STOCK, 62, PATERNOSTER ROW, E.C.
1896.

PREFACE.

THE author of these Historical Sketches has drawn his information from a variety of sources, only a few of the chief of which are indicated in the course of the narrative. Every care, however, has been taken to verify all statements. The portions of the work directly relating to Armenia and the Armenians have had the advantage of having been revised, as to facts and dates, by an Armenian scholar, an expert in this subject, as it was passing through the press.

He thus writes, at date, as to the present situation and cheerless outlook for his wretched countrymen : ' What about the next winter, when the snow once more cuts off communications and the Kurd and the Turk are the sole masters of the situation, without even a watching eye to disturb them ? . . . It makes one more than sick to think of it all.'

As these lines are being traced there are tragic indications of a revival of disturbances and massacres, which are the manifest result, in the first instance, of the misgovernment of the Grand

Turk, and in the next, of the apathy of the European concert.

The despatches just submitted to Parliament (Turkey, No. 6, 1896), while sufficiently emphasizing the mistaken policy of certain agitators for reform among the Armenians, yet present us with the most ghastly picture of provincial misrule as the real source of these terrible disorders.

Emphatic testimony is borne in these consular reports to the complicity of the government of the Sultan, whose deliberate policy, it is stated, is to crush and stamp out the Christian population of Asiatic Turkey.

In relation to this state of things, and in proof that the attitude of the present Prime Minister of England has not been misrepresented in these pages, and is still unchanged, we submit a few sentences from his latest utterances on this subject :

' I shall be informed that I have threatened the Ottoman Government, and am bound to carry the threats out. I entirely demur to that criticism. . . . A preacher may be very earnest in denouncing sin, but he is not bound to come down from the pulpit to take a big stick and inflict chastisement on the impenitent ; and, therefore, when I say that there is a gangrene in the extremity of Europe, do not assume that I am making any kind of implication that I intend to volunteer the *rôle* of physician to cut it out.'

A. O. I.

CONTENTS.

PART I.

ARMENIA AND THE ARMENIANS IN ANCIENT TIMES.

CHAPTER I.

PAGE

Geographical position of Ancient and Turkish Armenia —Historical sketch of the Armenians in earlier times   -   -   -   -   -   -   1—18

CHAPTER II.

The introduction of Christianity into Armenia as the national religion by St. Gregory the Illuminator and his successors in the fourth century—Constitution of the old Armenian Church   -   -   -   19—30

CHAPTER III.

Arsacidan and Sassanian dynasties—Religious and literary revival—Translation of the Scriptures by St. Miesrop and St. Isaac—Sketches of Armenian history from the introduction of Christianity by St. Gregory to the rise of the dynasty of the Bagratidæ, A.D. 860   31—5

CHAPTER IV.

PAGE

Dynasty of the Bagratidæ — Rupenian kingdom of
Cilicia — Relations with the Crusaders — Close of
Armenian monarchy   ·   -   -   - 51—60

PART II.

*ARMENIA AND THE ARMENIANS UNDER TURKISH
MISRULE—THE PRESENT CRISIS IN ARMENIA.*

CHAPTER I.

The Turks and Saracens—Seljouk Turks—Togrul Beg
—Rise of the Ottoman Empire—Fall of Constanti-
nople—Decline of the Ottoman Empire—Position of
Armenia -   -   -   -   -   - 61—76

CHAPTER II.

Islam as the religion of the Turk—Youth of Mahomet
—Mahomet at Mecca—Temptations of Mahomet—
The Sword and the Koran—Influence of Islam on
the character and government of the Turk—Forced
conversions   ·   ·   ·   ·   - 77—95

CHAPTER III.

Glimpses of Armenian life since the final overthrow of
the monarchy on to the beginning of the present century—Persian oppression—Shah Abbas—Armenian
patriarchs—Roman Catholic influence—Literary revival of the eighteenth century—Summary   - 96—104

Contents

CHAPTER IV.

PAGE.

Political situation in Turkey towards the close of the
last, and during the first half of the present, century
—Degeneracy of the Turk—Russian advances—Peter
the Great—Traditional policy of Russia—Reforming
Sultans - - - - - - 105—115

CHAPTER V.

New phases of the Armenian Question—Gradual change
of policy of the reforming Turk—Protestant influence
—American missions—Conflicting verdicts—Political
reforms reviewed—Treaty of Adrianople, 1829 —Hatti
Sherif, 1839—Protestant Charter, 1850—Hatti Humayoun in view of prospective demands of the Treaty
of Paris—Summary - - - - 116—127

CHAPTER VI.

European concert and its relation to Turkey—Treaty of
Paris, 1856—Turkish diplomacy—Young Armenia—
National Constitution (1862), and National Commission (1871) — Situation before the Treaty of San
Stefano—Cyprus Convention, and Treaty of Berlin
(1878)—Sixty-first and Sixty-second Articles—Peace
with Honour—Summary - - - 128—149

CHAPTER VII.

Position of Armenia after the Treaty of Berlin—Bright
prospects—Turkish reforms—Attitude of European
concert — Consular reports — Comments of British
press—Hamidieh cavalry—Sassoun massacres, 1894
—New reforms - - - - - 150—174

Contents

CHAPTER VIII.

PAGE

Renewal of massacres, 1895-96—The Hindchag's Communication to the Embassies—Collective Note—Illustrative cases—Trebizond and Ourfa—Attitude of Prince Lobanoff—Responsibility for the massacres—Relation of the European Powers—The special responsibility of Great Britain—Question not closed—Solutions of the problem—Conclusion -   - 175—200

ERRATA.

Page 27 (line 3) delete sentence beginning—' It is further, &c.'

Page 27 (line 13). For sentence beginning : The dioceses, &c. —read, ' The chief dignitaries of the Armenian Church are five—*viz.*, the patriarch of Etchmiadzin and Ardaghar in Greater, and Sis in Lesser Armenia, with the titular patriarchs of Constantinople and Jerusalem. The three first named also receive the title of Catholicos.

PART I.

ARMENIA AND THE ARMENIANS IN ANCIENT TIMES.

CHAPTER I.

Geographical position of Ancient and Turkish Armenia—
Historical sketch of the Armenians in earlier times.

THE regions lying in and around the north-east corner of Asia Minor possess a unique historical interest. They are the reputed home of the human race. Across their steppes, with herds and flocks, roamed the nomadic tribes of the patriarchal age. By-and-by comes a movement down to the plains. The arid uplands are exchanged for the fertile valleys of the great rivers.

With the set seasons of agriculture the roving life comes to an end. From the legal relations arising out of a fixed tenure of the land appears the first faint glimmering of citizenship and the State. Contact with the sea introduces a new element. Commerce assumes fresh aspects, and the development of the uplands and of the river valleys reaches its full maturity on the coast.

Here, then, through its three great stages, the advance of civilization has been carried forward. Even at the present day all three stages—the nomadic, the territorial, the maritime—can be found co-existing where Europe and Asia blend into each other.

On this borderland of two great continents were laid the opening scenes of that abrupt historical transition when, by the fall of Constantinople in 1453, the Middle Ages may be supposed to end and modern history to begin. It is with that part of these regions known from ancient times as Armenia, and with its relations to the surrounding countries, that we are now concerned.

It is certainly not the magnitude of the mother-country of the Armenians, for at no time have they possessed any vast territory ; it is not their numbers, for they have never been a great multitude—it is not on either of these accounts that they have come to occupy the prominent position they have held, and still continue to hold, in the history of the world. They have not, like their present masters, the Turks, mustered their hordes of lawless marauders ; they have not spread desolation along their line of march, nor have they set up a rival imperium to the great forces of modern civilization. Yet they assert a position of influence and inherit a prestige which never can be associated with the name of their barbarous oppressors.

Their peculiar claim to a place of honour among the nations lies in their distinctive genius and character, their realization of a principle of national unity, and of a high ideal as to their mission, to which they have clung amid every change, every reverse of fortune.

We purpose to note, however cursorily, some of
the moulding influences of this character, as well
as some of its heroic achievements.

It cannot, we believe, be without profit that we
tread, even in imagination, that ancient realm of
noble martyrdoms, of new-born aspirations, and
mark the recurring outflashes of spirit which lend
their mingled pathos and romantic charm to the
history of this remarkable nation.

Armenia looms forth from amid the mists of
antiquity a rugged, grim old fortress, often,
indeed, beleaguered, but never finally captured.

Ancient Armenia, in its palmiest days, according
to Moses of Chorene, overran, if it did not take
possession of, all the range stretching from the
Caspian to the Mediterranean Sea. That range
includes the wild fastnesses of the Caucasus, what
is now the Russian province of Georgia, the
mountains, plains and valleys of Turkish Armenia
and Anatolia, as well as the maritime regions of
the Euxine and the Bosphorus.

Turkish Armenia, to which we now confine our
survey, occupies the north-east corner of Asia
Minor. It is bounded on the north by the Black
Sea and the frontier of Russia, on the east by
Russia and Persia, on the west by Anatolia,
and on the south by the mountains of Kurdistan.
It is distant from Constantinople 600 miles. Its
extent from east to west is 430, and its breadth
from north to south 300 miles.

The original name Haiasdan was given to

it from the national progenitor, Haig, whom
tradition asserts to have been the son of
Togarmah, the grandson of Japhet.

Armenia (a later designation, derived, it is said,
from one of the old kings, Aram, a descendant of
Haig) is generally supposed to signify highland. It
is descriptive of the surface of the country, which is
mostly an elevated plateau, from 4,000 to 7,000 feet
above the level of the sea, sloping downwards towards Persia on the east, and Anatolia on the west.
Its aspect, in some of the mountain ranges, suggests
an expansion of the grandeur and beauty of the
Trossachs. Armenia contains large tracts of plain
and valley capable of a high degree of cultivation.
The Turkish despot, however, will do nothing worth
mentioning to encourage the rayah in his cultivation of the soil, even to enrich himself and his
rapacious pashas. The Armenian peasant, therefore, devoid of the appliances of science to his
occupation, does not thrive on agriculture.

The soil is rich in minerals such as coal, copper,
iron, lead, salt, and naphtha. These, however,
until quite recently, the unspeakable Turk would
neither work himself nor permit others more
competent to do so. Mr. Curzon, who comments
on the folly of this dog-in-the-manger policy,
bears ample testimony to the existence of boundless coal fields between the Bosphorus and
Heraclea, as well as to the facility with which the
coal cropping out of the sides of the hills could be
obtained.

The country, like the Highlands of Scotland, suffers from a scarcity of wood. The neglect of artificial means of irrigation condemns large portions of the soil to barrenness. But this is redeemed by the fertility of other regions. The products are rice, hemp, flax, cotton, tobacco, grapes, and a variety of fruits. Cattle-rearing is more in favour than agriculture.

The climate of Armenia is temperate and bracing. The Euphrates and Tigris are the principal rivers. Rising in its mountain fast-nesses, and uniting at last in the Shat-al-Arab, they pour their waters into the Persian Gulf.

In like manner, the Araxes and Kur, rising in the same centre, after traversing divergent routes, unite in discharging their waters in one vast volume into the Caspian Sea. Other streams, such as the Jorokh and Rion, or Phasis, drain Armenia in the direction of the Black Sea.

Along the banks of the two larger historic rivers, the Euphrates and Tigris, even in the absence of irrigation, vineyards and garden landscapes meet the eye, giving the observant student of Scripture some remote conception of the extent and delights of the far-off Edenic paradise.

The natural guardian of Armenia is Agri-dagh, or the ancient Ararat, rising in the east to the height of 17,260 feet. It is known among the natives and others as Noah's Mountain. A fondly cherished tradition declares that, in 'the untrodden solitude of Ararat's tremendous peak,' the ark may still be found embedded amid the eternal snows. It is quite clear that these primitive Orientals, wonderful as they were in many respects, had not foreseen what troubles their haphazard statements were laying up in store for the exercise of the patience and industry of the higher critics.

Somewhere in these regions which go by the name of Ararat, the ark, we may be permitted to suppose, did come to rest. Hence Armenia's claim to be, if not the first, at least the second cradle of the human race. The country east of the Euphrates, when most fully organized for political purposes, under a native dynasty, consisted of fifteen divisions. The original Armenia has now come to be portioned out as provinces of Turkey, Russia and Persia.

Turkish Armenia at the present day, including Kurdistan, forms a separate province of the Ottoman Empire. It is subdivided into three vilayets, or governments—Erzeroum, Mamouret-ul-Aziz, and Diarbekir—with the adjoining regions of Bitlis and Van. Erzeroum, the political capital of Turkish Armenia, is favourably situated for commercial and military purposes, being on the highway between the East and the West.* Van,

---

* Consul Hampson, writing from Erzeroum, December 19, 1891, says : ' As far back as the year 1850, Consul Brandt drew the attention of the Embassy to the existence of valuable coal mines in this neighbourhood. . . In spite of the fact, however, that fuel is one of the great difficulties at Erzeroum, both for household and manufacturing purposes, that wood is brought every year from greater distances, and,

one of the old capitals, is, from its associations
with native and Assyrian story, foremost in
romantic and antiquarian interest. Batoum,
along with Kars, was ceded to Russia by the
Berlin Treaty, 1878.

From the fluctuations of the limits of Armenia,
as we have now indicated, it is difficult, or rather
impossible, to mention boundaries of a fixed kind.
The region just described may be regarded as the
mother-country. It contains a mixed population
of Turks, Kurds, etc., and only about 600,000
Armenians, or about one-fourth of the whole
number within the Turkish dominions.

The Armenians at present are said to number
about four millions. Of these there are about
two and a half millions in Turkey, one and a
fourth millions in Russia, 150,000 in Persia and
the East, 100,000 in Europe, and 5,000 in the
United States of America.

The Armenians claim to be the oldest nation
on the face of the earth. They date the origin of
their dynasties from the time when the ark rested

consequently, continually increases in dearness, and that,
from this cause, the establishment of any machine-worked
industry is practically impossible here, the Government has
steadily refused all permission to exploit the coal which is
known to exist. . . . Nor is coal the only valuable natural
product thus neglected, although it is the one the necessity
for which is most pressing. I am assured that within a
radius of three miles from one of the coal fields exist rich
silver and copper mines, permission to work which has also
been refused. Gold and boracite have also been found in
the same district, and in another district a spring of petroleum
of excellent quality is known to exist.'—' Blue Book,' Turkey,
No. 3 (1896).

on the mountains of Ararat. They even go still further back, and claim that the Armenian was the language spoken in the Garden of Eden. They designate themselves Haik, after the great-grandson of Japhet, the reputed founder of their nation. The Armenians are no doubt, like other Aryan races, of the line of Japhet. They are distinguished by their native intelligence and spirit of enterprise. In these and other respects they resemble the Semitic character, and have often been compared with the Jews. There is a somewhat cynical proverb, that it takes two Jews to cheat a Greek, and two Greeks to cheat an Armenian.

The Armenian is of striking personal appearance, with keen, dark, flashing eyes and restless temperament; he is above the middle height; the complexion is darkish brown or yellow; the forehead is broad and massive.

We turn to the page of sacred history for the earliest reliable references to Armenia. There we learn that the ark rested on the mountains of Ararat. There are other and later references, as that to the sons of Sennacherib, who, after slaying their father in self-defence, escaped into Armenia. Both Ezekiel and Jeremiah refer to it—the one to its traffic in mules and horses with Tyre, the other to its alliance with Cyrus in the siege of Babylon.

The oldest native histories are to a large extent a mass of fable. Little more can be learned from them than that in ancient times the

Armenians were governed by independent or tributary kings, and that the Assyrians, the Medes, and Persians were in turn their conquerors and oppressors.

This fabulous history has, however, some passages of lively interest. Let us instance a few of them : Haig, their natural progenitor, was, it seems, a prodigy of valour and religious zeal. He slew the tyrant Belus, who was the first to introduce idolatry among mankind. He lived to a great age; the chronicler does not affect precision on the point, but thinks it was probably 500 years. Armenac, the son of Haig, had twelve brothers, named after the months of the year ; he had also twenty-four sisters, named after the hours of the day. Aram, from whom the Armenians are supposed by the romancer to get their name, was the first to raise his people to a position of renown among the nations.

One of the first historical personages to appear on the stage of ancient Armenia is no other than the famous Assyrian queen Semiramis. Those who may have chanced to harbour a vague fancy that Semiramis, from the masculine type of character, is an old-world hero, will have their minds disabused of that fallacy when we mention that she appears as a royal lover smit with the charms of the Armenian king Arah. She somewhat overdoes her part, and makes him a proposal of marriage. She offers him, along with herself, the Assyrian crown. Arah does not see his way to accept of his good fortune. The royal passion suddenly changes from love to revenge. She invades his kingdom at the head of her army, and to her great grief Arah is slain in battle.

To make what amends she now can, she transfers her affection to Arah's son and heir. She places him upon his father's throne. Thereafter the love-lorn warrior-queen, conceiving a liking for the climate and scenery of Armenia, turns it into a summer resort. The spot chosen for her residence is the romantic region in the neighbourhood of Lake Van. There she builds not only a royal palace or castle, but also the city of Van. This region she continues to frequent until she falls in battle fighting against her own son, and by the side of her ally, the son of the beloved Arah. To this day the name of Semiramis survives in local designations in this spot. The romance so far furnishes the key to the explorer of the inscriptions about Lake Van. It enables him to understand why those inscriptions are entirely different from the Persian or Babylonian character, and are mostly in the Assyrian style of cuneiform writing. The historians Diodorus Siculus and Strabo both confirm the accounts of monumental erections in Armenia by Semiramis.

About the time when the Israelites departed from Egypt, Armenia, we are told, was temporarily subdued by Sesostris, the Egyptian king. The reigning prince was then Pharnak, who soon regained his independence. In the time of his successor, Soor, took place the conquest of Canaan by Joshua. Many of the aboriginal Canaanites took refuge in Armenia. One of these old Armenian kings, named Zarmayr, was engaged in the Trojan war on the side of Priam, and was slain in single combat by Achilles. We have, however, no Homer to describe the encounter, or to rehearse the haughty colloquy which must have preceded it.

In the reign of Paroyr, who was a contemporary of Sennacherib of sacred history, Armenia threw off the Assyrian yoke, and joined Arbaces the Mede in his rebellion against Sardanapalus. On the murder of Sennacherib by his two sons, Adramelech and Sharezer, Paroyr received the parricides into his dominions. The allegiance of Armenia was now transferred to Media, the native dynasty still holding its place.

After another long list of mythical kings, we come to Haygag II. He was an ally of Nebuchadnezzar, King of Babylon. When the Jews were carried by this monarch into captivity, Haygag received into his kingdom a Jewish chief, Shambat, with his family. This Shambat and his posterity settled in the country, and his name is revered as the ancestor of the great dynasty of the Bagratidæ, which was destined in due time to occupy the throne of their adopted country.

During the period of Median supremacy there seems to have been a revival of the native spirit of independence. Tigranes I. distinguishes himself by a victory over the Median king Ahasuerus, whom he slays in battle with his own hand. The victory is also due largely to the self-sacrifice of Tigrana, a sister of the King of Armenia. The wedded queen of Ahasuerus, she divulges his evil designs against the throne of her brother, and flees for protection to her native country. The information had proved a timely warning, and Tigrana ranks henceforth among the saviours of Armenia. Not less interesting, and more authentic, is the record of the alliance of Tigranes with Cyrus, the Persian king, in the overthrow of Babylon, and the liberation of the Jews from captivity, B.C. 538. To this event Jeremiah is supposed to refer in the prophecy, ' Call together against her the kingdoms of Ararat, Minni and Askenaz . . . to make the land of Babylon a desolation without an inhabitant.'

According to the chronology of both Jews and Armenians, Tigranes was the Armenian king at the capture of Babylon. Under all these changes in her relations to her neighbours, Armenia continued to retain her native dynasties with more or less show of independence.

There are frequent allusions to Armenia in both the Institution and Expedition of Cyrus. In the year B.C. 401, the Armenian satrap Teribazus was startled by the approach of a vast body of armed men from the south, bent, as he could not doubt, on the invasion of his country. He prepared at once to contest their passage of the small river

Centrites, by which the Armenian frontier was bounded. After some encounters, it was found that the strangers harboured no designs on Armenia. The relations now changed, and the chief troubles of the retreating Ten Thousand arose, not from a hostile people, but from the rigours of an Armenian winter. The narrative of Xenophon, with its side-lights on the habits of life, the earth-dwellings and warlike character of the Armenians, is familiar to every reader of the Anabasis.

But a conqueror from the West did at last appear on the plains of Asia, through whom both the Persian and Armenian prestige was destined to receive a blow from which it was never fully to recover. Vahey, the last of the Armenian kings, and the ally of Darius, fell in battle, fighting bravely against the enemy. That enemy was no other than the victorious Alexander, the son of the Macedonian Philip. Armenia now became a Greek province. On the death of Alexander the Great (B.C. 323), it fell to the lot of one of his successors, Seleucus, and was thereupon ruled by the Syrian Seleucidæ, until B.C. 246. They were succeeded by the Arsacidæ, who founded the empire of the Parthians.

About B.C. 150, the Arsacidan or Parthian king, Arsaces the Great (Mithridates I.), placed his brother Valarsaces on the throne of Armenia. This monarch, after having made some important conquests, turned his attention to the administration of his dominions, and endeavoured to improve

the condition of his people. In this beneficent
labour he was ably assisted by Bagarat, his Jewish
minister, whose name was yet to become so prominent among the rulers of Armenia. The Arsacidan
or Parthian dynasty continued until A.D. 226.
This, again, was succeeded by that of the Sassanidæ, which ruled for over 400 years. The power
of the Arsacidæ over Armenia rose and fell with
the fortunes of Persia in her struggle with her formidable rivals. In these fluctuations the supremacy
of Rome asserted itself, and Armenia became a
Roman province. The raid of Antony into
Armenia, to humour the caprice of his mistress
Cleopatra, and the exhibition of an Armenian
king, in gilded chains, in the streets of Alexandria,
is a striking rather than influential episode in
the history of the country.

In the reign of Constantine the Great, Armenia
had acquired such a degree of independence, or,
in more modern phrase, Home Rule, as to have
its own tributary king.

We have thus briefly sketched the outline of
the earlier period of Armenian history.

The chief if not the only guides over this
period are the native writers—Moses of Chorene,
a disciple of Miesrop, belonging to the fifth century; and Father Michael Chamich, who published
his history of Armenia in 1786. The latter work
was translated into English by Johannes Avdall,
Calcutta, 1827. Mr. Avdall belongs to a small
yet distinguished group of native Armenian

scholars, who have in recent times done good service on behalf of the enlightenment of their own country and of the Eastern world.

The earlier of these two histories, that of the gentile Moses, extends from Haig, the great-grandson of Japhet, on to A.D. 440. His narrative must, from the lack of the necessary information, as there are no ancient records, be largely of a legendary character. A certain Syrian romancer, Mar Ibas by name, seems to have had sufficient resources to impose upon this lover of antiquarian lore, and to mislead him into the acceptance of much that was merest fable as veritable history. And yet one ought not to forget that the Armenian Moses did his best with an impossible task, and if he does not much instruct, can hardly fail, now and again, to amuse his reader.

As Father Chamich, whose history extends from B.C. 2247 to the year of Christ 1780, rests the earlier portion of his narrative on the authority of his predecessor, we cannot wonder that his record is not more successful. In the more clearly-defined historic period, at which it may be supposed we have now arrived, there are, of course, other guiding lights.

We have, however, reached the limits of what we had intended to say on the earliest times of Armenia.

An incursion has been made into an ancient realm which is not only the mother-country of the Armenians, but of the human race.

We cannot wonder that a halo of romance, in the absence of the clear light of history, should crown the brows of its hoary mountains, and spread itself over its plains and lakes, its cities and palaces.

As the enveloping mists from time to time roll away, we can see that the drama of Armenian life is no fiction, but a stern reality. To a closer scrutiny there are not wanting proofs of a progressive national movement. The Assyrian, the Egyptian, the Median, the Persian, the Greek and Roman conquerors march stormfully across the stage.

We see one ruthless hand after another made, in some degree, to relax its grasp of the victim, until at last a master appears, who can not only control, but also educate his vassal. With the conquest of the Greek Alexander, and the subsequent Roman domination, we enter upon a new era in the history of Armenia.

CHAPTER II.

THE culture and civilization of the West had begun to penetrate into Armenia with the victorious legions of the Greeks and Romans. Another of the many deluges which have swept over this unhappy land was showing tokens of subsidence, and the ark was once more nearing a place of rest.

The inauguration of this new era was the acceptance of the Christian religion as the national faith. This was the grand decisive event which was destined to draw forth the noblest qualities of the Armenian people, and to preserve to this day their national unity. Some conception of the character of this movement is thus necessary to enable us to understand their subsequent history. For the accounts we have of this change of the national religion, we are mainly indebted to the father of Armenian history— Moses of Chorene. His narrative is none the less valuable that we know it to be confirmed, in some portions, by collateral evidence.

The calendar of the Armenian Church records, giving specific dates, the casting of its founder, St. Gregory, into the pit, the taking of him out of it, and the finding of his body in Mount Sebuh. Chrysostom is one of his many panegyrists. A history of events from the time of Abgar, with a Life of St. Gregory, had been written by Agathangelos, but it is a tissue of fable. There is also a modern life in Armenian, by the Uniat Vartabed Matthew, translated into English by Rev. S. C. Malan, 1868. Even with these and such-like authorities we can hardly wonder that it is not always easy to say what is fact and what is fiction.

It is not possible to give specific information on the original forms of the religion of the race. They claim, indeed, for their ancestor the distinction of having slain Belus, the first propagator of idolatry. His descendants, however, would seem to have, in course of time, devised a religious cult of their own, as well as to have yielded so far to the idolatrous nature-worship of their neighbours. Immediately before the introduction of Christianity 'the prevailing religion was a mixture of Persian fire-worship and Greek idolatry.' To this, no doubt, we may add the worship of their own native divinities.

The Armenians were the first nation to accept the Christian religion. The Roman Empire was a full generation behind them in taking this step. Some thirty-seven years elapsed from the baptism of Tiridates, his household, courtiers and others, to the publication of the edict for the toleration of the new faith by the Roman Emperor.

The founder of the national Armenian Church had seen his wondrous visions of the Only Begotten, and built the Cathedral of Etchmiadzin, under the shadow of Mount Ararat, before Constantine, as the result of his vision of the luminous cross and its motto, had given instructions that it should replace the eagle on the standards of his armies. The ancient chroniclers claim for the Armenian Church an Apostolic origin and constitution. Abgar, the Arsacidan king, who reigned from B.C. 5 to A.D. 32, wrote, we are told, a letter to Jesus. The king requested the Saviour to cure him of some disease, and to come and live at his court. A reply was sent through the Apostle Thomas, assuring him of the cure of his distemper, and promising him in due time spiritual life for himself and his people.

In fulfilment of this promise, it is related Thaddeus, Bartholomew, and Jude preached the Gospel and suffered martyrdom in Armenia.

Legend apart, it is not unlikely that the Gospel was preached in Armenia by some of the converts of the Apostolic Churches of Asia Minor, either in the first or second century. But there is sufficient evidence that, under the persecutions which followed, the people again fell back into idolatry.

The revival of the faith, culminating in a permanent national acceptance, dates from the time of St. Gregory, the Illuminator of all Armenia. His Armenian epithet is Lusavoritch, Greek Photistes. St. Gregory was the youngest son of an Arsacidan prince, Anak, who mortally stabbed the reigning Armenian king, Chosroes, A.D. 232. The dying king ordered the instant slaughter of his murderer and all his family. At this critical juncture took place the birth of Gregory, the youngest son of the doomed household. The child was preserved by the devotion of his nurse, a Christian woman, who got him conveyed to the protection of a Christian noble of Cæsarea, called Euthalius. Here he was educated in the faith of the Gospel. Afterwards he carried on his studies in Athens and Rome. Returning to Cæsarea, he married a lady like-minded with himself. We are told that her name was Mary, and that she was the mother of two sons, destined to do noble service to the cause of Christ in Armenia. The narrative goes on to say that three years after the birth of her youngest son she and her husband separated by mutual consent, to serve God by a closer union. She spent the rest of her life in a nunnery. Whatever may be said of this story, the Armenian Church does not enjoin celibacy upon its priesthood. St. Gregory's experience may thus have taught him a useful lesson, from which others were to profit in the years to come. Free from family ties, imbued with the culture of Greece and

Rome, and, above all, burning with Apostolic zeal
for the spread of the Gospel among his countrymen, Gregory returned to Armenia. Preserving
his incognito for a time, he gained admission into
the royal household, and established himself in the
favour of King Tiridates, the son of the murdered
Chosroes. Tiridates was a violent persecutor of
the Christians. It had been his great object to
utterly exterminate the few still to be found in his
kingdom.

Not aware of the creed of Gregory, Tiridates
had ordered him to crown his favourite goddess,
Anahit, with garlands. Gregory avowed his faith
in Christ, and boldly refused to participate in
idolatry. Tiridates subjected him, it is said, to
twelve different species of torture, and finally cast
him into a noisome pit. He remained in prison
for thirteen, some say fifteen years.

At length St. Gregory, having cured the king or
his sister of a terrible disease, was set at liberty.
He at once began to preach the Gospel. He now
numbered among his converts the persecutor
Tiridates himself, his queen, and his sister. Of
the last it is naively said by the historian that she
was a remarkable woman, who 'did not, like other
females, let loose her tongue, even when she was
not a Christian.'

Agathangelos says, mistaking a parable for a
merely grotesque miracle, that the king was
transformed into a boar, and came to the feet
of St. Gregory, who restored him to his original

form. The change was no doubt typical of that
which passed on many others as well as the king.
Brutal ferocity began to give place to the supremacy of a new spirit. It has ever been the glory
of the Gospel of Christ that its strains have
effectually subdued and softened wilder and more
savage natures than were wont to be swayed by
the lyre of Orpheus.

How far the conversion of the nation was a real
transformation of character we cannot say.

The courtiers, so far as outward conduct went,
largely followed the example of the king. The
movement became national. The notions of pro-
pagating religion in those early times were not
what, under a better understanding of its spirit,
they have since become. The primitive African
chief, who ruled his tribesmen by club-law alone,
could not understand why the missionary should
trouble himself reasoning with and exhorting them
to receive the Gospel. All that was necessary, as
it seemed to him, was to send round among them
a peremptory order, to be enforced, if need be, by
the headsman's application of the cowhide.

The same rough-and-ready method for the defence and propagation of the Gospel has ever had
its attractions for not a few, since Peter first drew
his sword against his Master's foes in the Garden
of Gethsemane. But it has not been resorted to
by our wisest reformers. St. Gregory was a true
Christian missionary. Brave in suffering, diplomatic in action, considerate and generous in deal-

ing with the prejudices and foibles of men, he saw
that the revolution at which he aimed could only be
effected by spiritual forces. These he could exercise
and utilize with a genius and energy all his own.

At the desire of Tiridates, Gregory went to
Cæsarea, and was there, A.D. 302, consecrated
by Leontius, the Archbishop, Patriarch of all
Armenia. He then set himself to organize the
new Church, and to establish a system of schools.

He gathered together a number of rough country
boys, and instructed them particularly in the knowledge of the Scriptures. His presence and teaching
wrought a marvellous change upon their characters.
They saw him setting aside every consideration of
ease and safety in the pursuit of his mission. No
service was too lowly or trying for him to render
to others; no opposition could quench or even
damp his enthusiasm. The priests of the decaying idolatry received his instructions and proffered their services the more gladly that he was
careful of their worldly interests and continued
to them their former emoluments.

Having completed the magnificent temple of
The Only Begotten at Etchmiadzin, and carried
through what personal service he could render to
the cause to which he had devoted his life, St.
Gregory, now an aged man, retired to Mount
Sebuh, to end his days in solitary communion
with God. His son had already been appointed
as his successor at Etchmiadzin.

He died alone, unattended. The body was

covered with a heap of stones by some shepherds about the mountain. Some years afterwards it was removed, and laid to rest in the village of Thorkan, in Mount Sebuh.

Since then, tradition assures us, the sacred body of St. Gregory has been distributed over a large area of Christendom. The head and prison-chains were conveyed to Naples; the left hand was conveyed to Etchmiadzin, and the right to Sis.

Under such circumstances did the Church of St. Gregory—the most ancient of national Christian Churches—find a place in Armenia. The central temple stands where it has stood since the days of its founder, at Etchmiadzin, at the base of Ararat, in the fertile valley of Erivan in Upper Armenia. It has belonged since 1828 to the Russian division of Armenia. It is the residence of the chief patriarch of the Armenian Church. His title, no doubt somewhat more complex since the simple times of St. Gregory, runs thus : ' The servant of Jesus Christ, and by the grace of God Catholicos of all the Armenians, and Patriarch of the Holy Convent of Etchmiadzin.'

The list of the successors of the first patriarch is of great length, extending from his son Aristaces on to the present day, and to his Holiness Mugerditch Khrimian, the present Catholicos of Etchmiadzin. He is represented as a man of large and liberal views, anxious for a progressive movement. As one glances over the Armenian Church calendar, he is struck not only by the array of sacred feasts, but also by their frequent and severe fasts.

The form of government is episcopal. The chief patriarch is chosen by the representatives of the dioceses, met in regular synod at Etchmiadzin. The nomination is then submitted to the Emperor of Russia, who, when he gives his approval, notifies the appointment to the Governments of Turkey and Persia. The chief dignitaries of the Armenian Church are five—viz., the patriarchs of Etchmiadzin and Ardaghar in Greater, and Sis in Lesser, Armenia, with the titular patriarchs of Constantinople and Jerusalem. The three first named also receive the title of Catholicos.'*

There are two religious orders of men among the Armenians: one follows the rule of St. Anthony, the other that of St. Basil. The robing of the priests when about to celebrate the Eucharist is a highly symbolical ceremony.

The Armenian Liturgy is regarded as one of the most ancient and beautiful of its kind. It was compiled originally from liturgies used by St. Gregory, St. Basil, and St. Athanasius. It was revised, in the fifth century, by the translators of the Scriptures into the Armenian tongue. The liturgy regulates the Communion Service.

* Dr. Wilson's 'Lands of the Bible' (Armenian Church), vol. ii., pp. 481, 482.

That service is conducted with an attention to elaborate ceremonial which has well-nigh turned the heads of some of our English ritualists who have witnessed its observance.

The National Church of Armenia was soon tested by a bloody persecution. In the reign of Julian the Apostate it so pressed upon the people that many of them relapsed into heathenism. The nobles drove from the throne Chosnes, the son of Tiridates. Then followed an ordeal of suffering in which nearly all the prelates and priests were martyred, including Husak, son of Vertannes, the Patriarch of Armenia.

In A.D. 345 Chosnes was restored to the throne, and Christianity made a further advance as the national religion. From A.D. 364, when Arsaces, King of Armenia, created Nierces, the grandson of Husak, Primate of Armenia, Etchmiadzin became the seat of an independent hierarchy.

The translation of the Scriptures, which belongs to a still later period, may be said to have completed the national revolution. That revolution was not, indeed, the work of any one man, or even generation of men, but rather of a succession of national reformers.

The Armenian Reformation, which we have been chiefly considering, was an event for which there had been a long Providential preparation. It is one of those formative periods of history which powerfully impress the student with the conviction of a Divine idea, working with creative energy, amid the seemingly aimless commotions of individuals and communities. Nothing can well be a more striking illustration of the guiding principle which constitutes the philosophy of history.

Yet the principle in question is ordinarily embodied in the person and career of either a single individual or cluster of individuals, and so the history of the great movements of the world is, at bottom, the history of its great men. In this sense the story of St. Gregory is largely, for this period, the story of Armenia. In it also we find the key to much otherwise utterly unintelligible in its subsequent history.

We have therefore traced the general course of this life-story. The scenes have flitted across the canvas somewhat swiftly and indistinctly. Yet the central figure has been ever before us.

First it is that of a helpless, doomed Armenian child, saved from the family massacre by a kind-hearted Christian nurse. In the next stage, we have an eager student of Western culture and the Scriptures in Cæsarea, the city of Cornelius and of the imprisonment of the Apostle of the Gentiles. In the third stage he steps forth a daring witness for Christ at the heathen court of one of the most relentless of the Armenian persecutors of the faith. In the last stage he appears as the Illuminator, carrying the light of the Gospel into all the dark corners of his native land. Never since

that time has this light wholly faded. The life-
story of this, the grandest of all the Armenian
saints, is an abiding record of labour, suffering,
and success. Every step of the Apostolic career
is full of interest, until the figure vanishes from
our view into its quiet devotional retreat in the
solitudes of Mount Sebuh.

Thus far the story of the founder of the national
Church of Armenia.

We have also glanced at that old Armenian
Church itself, its origin and constitution. We
have tried to see it at the far-off end of a long
retrospective vista, and before it had become, to
some degree, changed for good or evil by those
testing experiences through which it has since been
destined to pass.

CHAPTER III.

Arsacidan and Sassanian dynasties—Religious and literary revival—Translation of the Scriptures by St. Miesrop and St. Isaac—Sketches of Armenian history from the introduction of Christianity by St. Gregory to the rise of the dynasty of the Bagratidæ, A.D. 860.

WE can only glance rapidly at some of the more important events and tendencies in the history of Armenia during this period. In the absence of reliable information, largely accounted for by the unhappy circumstances of the country and people, that history, even at its best, is to some extent mythological. The principal native chronicler, Father Chamich, when he is not compiling a somewhat dry catalogue of Armenian kings, princes, and military chiefs, not to mention patriarchs and priests, is wont to regale his persevering reader with wonderful stories of supernatural agencies. If there is too frequently a monotonous repetition of calamity upon calamity, like a succession of wave-lines on mid-ocean, there is, at the same time, the most piquant variety in the standing miracles which embellish the national record.

The storms which swept over ancient Armenia, with tornado-like violence, buried among their débris large portions of the national record. While we have here and there a chapter of horrors which seems, somehow, like a facsimile of a former chapter in the long-drawn-out tragedy, there are not a few manifestly missing. Others are so blotted and blurred with blood and tears as to be far less decipherable than those strange runic characters on the rocks about Lake Van which have so severely taxed the ingenuity and patience of the disciples of Rawlinson and Layard.

But we return to our sketch. We have seen how the Armenian Church, the oldest national Church in Christendom, was founded by the Apostolic St. Gregory. We have traced some of his more immediate reforms, in which he was assisted so nobly by his royal convert Tiridates.

Tiridates was certainly one of the bravest and best of all the race of the Arsacidan kings which ruled over Armenia. When nearing the close of a long and brilliant career, seeing the Armenian chiefs relapsing into their former idolatrous habits and abandoning the sanctity of the Christian faith, Tiridates convened them together and remonstrated with them on their apostasy. As this produced no good results, he resigned the sceptre, and retired to spend the rest of his days on Mount Sebuh, where St. Gregory had passed in devout

seclusion the last years of his life. His turbulent
courtiers urged him in vain to resume the reins of
government, and exasperated by his persistent
refusal, they put an end to his life by poison.

So fell the first Christian King of Armenia, a
martyr to the faith of which at one time he had
been the most relentless persecutor. He died in
the eighty-fifth year of his age, and after a reign
of fifty-six years. His body was interred in the
fortress of Ani, a name which also recalls what
was for long afterwards one of the royal cities of
Armenia.

We may, perhaps, as well here indicate the
position and duration of the two main dynasties
which belong to this period, *i.e.*, those of the Arsacidæ and Sassanidæ. Some idea of their general
position and character is desirable for a better
understanding of their influence in Armenia. The
Arsacidan or Parthian dynasty succeeded that of
the Seleucidæ in the East, B.C. 246. It became
extinct in Persia A.D. 226. The Arsacidæ are
said by Father Chamich to have been of the
race of Abraham through Keturah. Gibbon
describes them as an obscure horde of Scythian
origin from all the provinces of Upper Asia.
They were beyond doubt a bold, warlike dynasty,
not much concerned about any form of religion,
and so, while subduing the Persians, did not much
interest themselves in their fire-worship. Their
successors, the Sassanidæ, claimed to be of
the ancient blood royal of Persia, and with

3

them it was a sacred mission to revive and
extend the faith of Zoroaster. This will explain
how it comes to pass that the fiercest and most
bloody religious persecution in Armenia was
carried on by the Sassanidæ, whose object was to
convert the Armenian nation to this alien creed.

Now, the Arsacidan dynasty, which occupied
the Persian throne until A.D. 226, was long survived by its offshoot which ruled in Armenia.
The latter was the tributary dynasty of the
former, which regarded Armenia as a province
of its empire. This relation it still held to Persia
after the accession of the Sassanian dynasty
to the Persian throne. The Sassanian Kings of
Persia accordingly sanctioned the appointment of
Arsacidan sovereigns in Armenia, and this went
on until the deposition of the last Arsacidan
Armenian monarch, Arlashir, by the Persian king
Baharam V. (Chamich, Viram) in A.D. 428. The
Sassanidæ continued to reign in Persia until they
were overthrown by the Saracens on the plains of
Cadesia in A.D. 636.*

During the reign of these Persian dynasties
they assumed an over - lordship of Armenia
and its tributary kings. When at length the
semblance even of monarchy disappeared with
the last Arsacidan King of Armenia, the op-

---

* ' Who on Cadesia's bloody plains
    Saw fierce invaders pluck the gem
    From Iran's broken diadem,
    And bind her ancient faith in chains.'
              Moore's ' Fire-worshippers.'

pression of the Sassanidæ became more intolerable, and a new era of endurance opened up for
the subject country.

Before we proceed to this stage, we must again
retrace our steps and note some earlier occurrences.   On the death of Tiridates and the settlement of his son, Khosrove II., by Greek force on
the throne of Armenia, a fierce war broke out
between the new sovereign and Sapor (Chamich,
Shapuh), which resulted in bloody engagements,
and was continued, on one pretext or another,
over the reigns of two other Armenian kings,
Tiran and Pap.   The character of the Armenian
kings down to the close of the fourth century is
such as modifies our regret that we do not know
more about them.   They were manifestly a rather
low type—sensual, perfidious and cruel.

But if the palaces of Armenia were not during
this period abodes of either virtue or piety, such
the Chronicler assures us was not the case with
the dwellings of the patriarchs and higher priesthood. This testimony is all the more pleasing
since after-ages have so often had too good reason
to comment on the degeneracy of the patriarchate, through the degradations to which,
especially under Moslem tyranny, it has been
systematically subjected.

In Armenia, as elsewhere, the Christian religion
has been the source of all the great movements
which elevate and consolidate a nation.   The
revolution originating with the primary labours of

St. Gregory was taken up by his son, St.
Vertannes, amid increasing difficulties. It found
a champion worthy to take the place of Gregory
himself in Nierses, one of the grandest pro-
phetic characters in Church history. While an
apostate race of sovereigns were living in open
debauchery, and cultivating alliances with the
infidel Julian, St. Nierses and some other like-
minded men were carrying through the stupendous
enterprise of what was in reality a second reformation in Armenia.   St. Nierses was appointed Patriarch of Armenia in A.D. 366. The Church became
at once a centre of new life. The mode of worship,
its outward forms, and, above all, its spirit, were
improved.   Convents were built to the number of
2,000, when the ideal of monastic life had not yet
been degraded by the corruptions of after-times.
Public schools, asylums for widows and orphans, as
well as other beneficent institutions, began to rise
over the land.   A true patriot, Nierses again and
again risked his life to deliver his country from
trouble incurred by its foolish rulers in their relations with the Greeks or Persians.   He fell at last
a martyr to the cause which he had served with
such unwearied devotion.

Having ventured to admonish the reprobate
King Pap for the betrayal of his faith, that miscreant secretly put him to death by poison. We
can hardly wonder that to the glowing imagination of his co-patriots and co-religionists a vision
of unearthly glory seems ever to surround the

person of such a man, and that at last it was
averred that he had been seen ascending to heaven,
accompanied by a host of angels.

Yet all this Christian activity was little else
than the prelude to greater and more enduring
labours. This was the religious and literary revival
connected with Miesrop, the secretary, and St.
Isaac, the son, of Nierses. St. Isaac became
Patriarch of Armenia in A.D. 390. In A.D. 393 he
began, in conjunction with Miesrop, a movement
for the improvement of the vernacular language.
Hitherto the Armenian had possessed no native
characters. In the east they employed the Persian,
and in the west of Armenia the Syriac, character.
The chronicle relates that St. Isaac and Miesrop
having both failed to do what they had purposed,
i.e., to invent a native alphabet, Miesrop went to
Somosata. In the act of prayer, so runs the
legend, he received the necessary help, and, rising
from his knees, he at once invented all the Armenian characters in exquisite perfection. This historical event, however mixed with fabulous details,
took place in A.D. 406. When the invention was
made public there were great rejoicings in Armenia.
St. Miesrop was borne in triumph into the capital,
and public thanks were returned to the Bestower
of all good. The new alphabet was now taught
in the schools.

Thus, as is ever the case, the Christian religion
brought with it a new intellectual era. Before
this time the Armenians had got what little culture

they had from the Assyrians and Medo-Persians.
But except a few old songs and ballads, the pre-
Christian literature of Armenia has ceased to exist.

The surviving literary treasures are thus subsequent to the fourth century, and are largely
historical. Poetry and fiction have not been
much cultivated by the Armenians. They are
a practical rather than a sentimental race,
receiving from those who know them best in
the business of life the designation of the Dutch-
men of the East, and this practical cast of
thought and utterance is characteristic of their
literary efforts. Their native tongue, or the old
Armenian, belongs to the Indo-Germanic group of
languages. It has no distinction of genders, and
abounds in irregularities of declension and conju-
gation ; has, it seems, a harsh sound, and is the despair of the foreigner as to mastery of pronuncia-
tion. With the impulse derived from Christian
thought, the Armenians now began to study the
works of the Greek philosophers and historians, the
masterpieces, indeed, of both Greek and Roman
culture, and to admire and copy these models.*

* Speaking of St. Miesrop, Mr. Tozer says : ' His name,
though little known in Europe, is still in great repute in his
native country, and with good reason ; for if any holy men
deserve to be held in pious remembrance, those have an
especial claim who, like Ulfilas, the Apostle of the Goths,
and Cyril and Methodius, the Apostles of the Slavonians,
and Miesrop, have invented alphabets for those among whom
they preached the Gospel. In their time and for the nations
they evangelized, they did hardly a less important work than
the inventors of printing subsequently did for the world at
large. From a political point of view, also, St. Miesrop

A few of their more promising disciples were now despatched by St. Miesrop and St. Isaac to Edessa and Constantinople to translate into Armenian some of the learned works of other nations. There they found and brought back with them to their masters a correct version of the Septuagint. Up to this time the Syrian version of the Bible had been used in Armenia, and an interpreter was needed to translate into the vernacular the portions of Scripture read at public worship.

This translation of the Scriptures into the Armenian tongue contains more books than those of the Western Churches. These additional books in the Old Testament are : (1) The Testament of the Twelve Patriarchs, the sons of Jacob ; (2) The History of Joseph and his wife Asenath ; (3) The Book of Jesus, the son of Sirach. In the New Testament the additions are : (1) The Epistle of the Corinthians to St. Paul ; (2) St. Paul's Third Epistle to the Corinthians. These additional books are considered apocryphal.

The Bible so translated into the vernacular is the oldest Armenian book extant, the next being that of Moses of Chorene, which was composed about half a century later. It is the crown of all the literary labours of the period to which it

was a great benefactor to his countrymen, for, whereas, up to that time, from the absence of a native version of the Scriptures and liturgy, they had been ecclesiastically, and to some extent politically, subject either to the Greeks or the Syrians, they were thenceforward able to assert their independence.' (Tozer's ' Turkish Armenia,' pp. 252, 253.)

belongs.   All agree that it is the highest model of
literary style. ˙ Thus, the Armenian version of
the Scriptures holds the same relative place to
other works as the version of Luther in Germany,
or the Authorized Version in our own country.

As the literary movements advanced, transla-
tions were made of such works as the Chronicles
of Eusebius, the Discourses of Philo, the Homilies
of St. Chrysostom, Servianus, Basil the Greek, and
Ephraim the Syrian.   Among the more prominent
literati who composed or translated were David,
the translator and commentator of Aristotle ;
Esnik, the author of certain works against the fire-
worshippers; Goriun, the Xenophon of Armenian
literature, the biographer of Miesrop.   Moses of
Chorene and Elisæus, a disciple of Miesrop, are
the chief native historians of this period.

The Armenians were now the foremost Christian nation in a double sense.   They were experi-
encing the beneficial effects of a revival of their
national faith.   But a testing ordeal was at hand.
We have said that the Arsacidan dynasty was not
to be regarded as an enthusiastic defender of the
creed of Zoroaster.   It was not a life purpose with
them to impose it on their Armenian or other subjects.   This temper changed at once with the accession of the Sassanidæ.   Their first sovereign,
Ardisher (Roman, Artaxerxes), succeeded in pro-
curing the assassination of Khosrove, the Arsacidan
King of Armenia, by Anak, the father of St. Gregory.
His son Tiridates would never have come to the

throne of Armenia had not the opposition of the
Sassanian king been overborne by the Greek
legions. All through their connection with this
Persian dynasty the Armenians were ever turning
for succour to their co-religionists at Constantinople. Bound together by a common creed, and
by the recent acceptance by both of the decrees
of the Council of Nice, A.D. 325, they often
took the field side by side in opposition to the
grand scheme of the Sassanian kings. That
scheme, as we have already said, was to convert Armenia to the religion of the Magi. The
persecution which thus ensued was not that of
a single despot, but of a whole Magian dynasty,
renewed at intervals over four centuries, and em-
bittered from the peculiar relation of the oppressor
and the oppressed, beyond all precedent, during
the latter half of this period. Among the Persian
kings most prominent in these bloody persecutions were Sapor ; Yezdejirt I. and II., in whose
reigns the atrocities were again revived ; and
Baharam V. (Chamich, Viram II.), who deposed
the last Arsacidan King of Armenia.

The resistance of the Armenian nation to these
long-continued attacks on their faith gives to this
whole otherwise doleful era in their history the
distinction of noble martyrdom, demanding the
most heroic courage and devotion. Armenia thus
stands forth as an Eastern realm which could not
be coerced into an alien faith either by the
scimitar of the Persian or the sword of Mahomet.

As we cannot go into details with this recital, we select a single persecution for a passing reference, as a specimen of many others, and of the spirit in which they were met by the Armenians.

Yezdejirt II., A.D. 450, had finally resolved that if oppressive taxation, torture, or any other of the approved weapons of Oriental imperialism, could accomplish it, Armenia must be made to embrace the Persian religion. The experiment, hitherto, had failed.* At length the despot wrote a letter, peremptorily demanding submission, and sent along with it an exposition of the tenets of the Magian creed. The demand was considered in an assembly of the chiefs and people convened by the pontiff St. Joseph in the city of Artashat. The assembly decided on a resolute rejection of the infamous injunction. The enraged king summoned the recalcitrant chiefs to his court, and threatened to send them in chains as exiles into a distant land, if they did not worship the sun on the following morning. Hoping to escape by a compromise, they did so—thinking this meantime the best course—to enable them ultimately to abide by the cause of their religion. On their return to their own country, they did not consider themselves bound by a concession wrung from them by tyrannical force. Under their leader Vartan they took the field against the invading Persian host, and fought with such valour that they completely routed the enemy. They de-

* See Neander's 'Church History,' vol. iii., pp. 149-152 ; also p. 161.

molished the fire temples, and rebuilt the profaned
and ruined churches. The brave Vartan. performed prodigies of valour; 'wherever he presented himself, the enemy were mowed down by
his sword, as blades of grass by the sickle,' but ere
the struggle was over he fell with nine other chiefs.

Thus the remorseless conflict went on, the
Armenians ever presenting, as a nation, a resolute
front to the foe. Towards the close of the sixth
century, Vahan, a Christian prefect, was appointed, and the Christian religion regained its
legitimate place in the nation.* At this temporary resting-place, we shall now note the position
of the Armenian Church, as regards her relation
to the Greek and Roman communions, and also
to the heresies of this period.

The harassed condition of the country, both in
Eastern and Western Armenia, continued under
the entire sway of the Sassanidæ, and was only
intensified by the Saracen invasions which then
took place, on to the close of the Saracenic rule
and the rise of the Bagratian dynasty. These
incessant national troubles account for the fact
that during the four centuries which follow the
golden age of Armenian literature there is little
or no intellectual advance. This condition of
mental torpor, due to the political circumstances
of Armenia, was also in part the cause and in
part the consequence of the rise of heresies and
divisions in the national Church. These arose
largely from the ignorance of the Church leaders.

* Chamich, vol. i., p. 323.

The Armenian Church remained in touch with the orthodox Greek and Latin Churches until the Council of Chalcedon, 451—the fourth General Council. The proceedings of this Council were fraught with disaster to the Armenian Church. The decrees of the three first Councils had been accepted by the Church of St. Gregory. Owing to a mistaken translation or some other cause, the Armenian Church condemned the decrees of the Council of Chalcedon, on the assumption that they tolerated or approved the Nestorian and Eutychian heresies. This condemnation was finally and formally made at the Synod of Thevin, 536. It has thus ever since underlain a plausible charge of heresy. Hence we trace the first stages of the schism which in 551 clove asunder the ancient Armenian Church into the two sections of the Church of St. Gregory and the Georgian Church. The latter removed the ban from the Council of Chalcedon, and so came into line with the Greek Church.

The Eastern and Western Armenian Churches were still further separated by some changes of ceremonial. The Western section began to use leavened bread and to mix the wine with water in the Eucharist. They also changed their Christmas Day to December 25, at the same time adopting some other innovations.*

---

* About this time, *i.e.* 562, the Armenian calendar was remodelled, and this date was fixed as the commencement of a new Haican era.

In order to understand the distinctive types of thought in the Eastern and Western Churches, and even the special heresies to which they gave rise, we must take into account the character and training of those who constituted their communions.

The Roman mind had for ages found the fullest exercise of its activities in the study of law. These habits of thought were brought to the problems of theology.

This peculiar influence was apparent in their first doctrinal discussions, and has continued to characterize those of subsequent times, as may be seen in the two great theological systems of the West, Arminianism and Calvinism, in regard to which it has been said, that it would be difficult to decide which is the more markedly legal in its tone.

Obligation, restitution, atonement, man everywhere in his legal relationships, such were the questions with which the Western Church chiefly busied herself. Far different were the problems which were moved in the Eastern Communion. The nature of the Godhead, the Divine attributes, the person of Christ, such were the subjects of eager and often bitter discussion in her councils.

Two distinct tendencies ere long appeared. The one, concentrating exclusively on the human, lost sight of the divine; the other, concentrating on the divine, lost sight of the human.

It was to the latter of these tendencies that
the Armenian Church had now inclined.*

The fortunes of Armenia were now to be influenced by a new power, to which allusion has
already been made, replacing that of the Sassanidæ, at Bagdad, in A.D. 637. This was the
dominion of the Saracens—a general designation
of the Greeks and Romans for the tribes inhabiting
Arabia. Nothing is more striking, more of the
essence of historical romance, than the origin and
rapid advance of this new race of conquerors—
the followers of their prophet Mahomet. When
Mahomet died in A.D. 632, Arabia had been subdued.
In the course of less than a generation, and within
the reign of the first four caliphs, his successors,
Syria, Persia and Egypt had also been conquered.

* 'One of the Vartabéds here [Uchkeliseh] . . . . introduced, of his own accord. the monophysitism of his Church,
by declaring that it receives only the first three of the
General Councils. Nestorius, he said, held to a perfect
separation of the Divinity and humanity of Christ, and
Eutyches taught that his humanity is absorbed in his
Divinity. The Armenians, agreeing with neither, believe
that the two natures are united in one, and anathematize all
who hold to a different creed. In this he spoke advisedly,
for it is well known that Eutyches is acknowledged by
neither of the three monophysite sects—the Armenian, the
Jacobite Syrian, and the Coptic, including the Abyssinian,
to which his controversy gave birth—and that his alleged
dogma of a confusion in the natures of Christ is the reason
of his rejection, though, perhaps, a candid investigation will
hardly find him chargeable with such an opinion. Another
intelligent ecclesiastic had told us that not only does his
nation hold to one nature, but also to only one will, in
Christ, thus making the Armenians partake in the mono-
thelite as well as in the monophysite heresy.'—Smith and
Dwight, ' Researches,' pp. 419-421.

The internal dissensions of the faithful, dividing
them so early into Sunis and Shias (the latter of
whom do not recognise the first three caliphs as
true successors of the Prophet), did not prevent
them from at once entering upon a course of
conquest unrivalled in the history of the human
race.   We cannot here further describe this movement, as it spread eastward and westward, and
threatened to revolutionize the history of the
world.

The first conquest outside of Arabia—that of
Syria—was also the first stroke dealt by the
Saracens to the prestige of the old Greek Empire.
The occupant of the throne of the Cæsars—
Heraclius—saw the victorious Omar establish his
Syrian capital at Damascus, amid indescribable
carnage, in A.D. 636. Jerusalem was already in
the hands of the infidel, and in A.D. 637 the
Mosque of Omar was erected on the site of the
ancient Jewish Temple.   In the same year the
Saracens, under their leader Abdorrahman, invaded Armenia, and imposed a tax on the
males of the district of Taron, carrying away
wives and children into captivity.   The atrocities
were renewed three years later, and such was the
devastation of the whole country that the pontiff
Ezr died heart-broken for the sorrows of Armenia.
The sack of Duin about this date recalls the
horrors of the destruction of Jerusalem and the
massacres of more modern times.   Twelve thousand of its citizens were cruelly butchered, and

thirty-five thousand taken captive. For fully another generation there was a ceaseless and bloody struggle for the mastery of Armenia between the Saracen and the Greek emperors.

In A.D. 685, Ashot, a Bagratian chief, became Governor of Armenia, and made peace with the Saracens. Two years later the Saracens assumed the government of Armenia. In A.D. 704 one of their former oppressors, Abdullah, became Caliph of Damascus, and inflicted terrible sufferings on the Armenians.

In A.D. 743 the Saracens built Bagdad, levying heavy taxes on the Armenians in aid of this undertaking. To Bagdad, soon after, the caliphate was removed. From this new centre were sent forth a succession of merciless tyrants to perpetrate every description of Moslem crime on their miserable victims.

In A.D. 849 Armenia revolted from its Saracen masters. This was followed by a series of massacres, which may well rank side by side with the most tragic occurrences in the history of this ill-fated country.*

* See Father Chamich's History, vol. i., p. 404: 'He directed (Bulah) to march immediately into Armenia to take vengeance for the late defeat. Bulah also received orders to seize all the Armenian chiefs and send them in chains to Bagdad, and to kill all whom he found in a condition to carry arms. Any of the people, however, who consented to forsake Christianity and embrace the religion of the Saracens he received directions to spare, provided they were strong and handsome. If they were homely, notwithstanding their inclination to abjure their religion,

In due time a better relationship was established between Armenia and its superior, the
Caliph of Bagdad, resulting in the change of
government which will be considered in our next
chapter.

The student of this period will find a suggestive
theme in tracing the course of Armenian influence in connection with the rise and progress
of the Byzantine Empire, from the time of
Leo III., its first sovereign, and the founder of
the Isaurian dynasty. Leo was himself a native
of Armenia. From his time Armenians became a
dominant power around the throne in Constantinople. Leo was the first Christian sovereign
who arrested the tide of Mohammedan conquest.
From the time of Heraclius the Roman Empire
had seemed hastening to hopeless ruin. Leo
has earned a right to be regarded as its saviour.
He reorganized its government, corrected abuses
in Church and State, and, in short, infused such
life into all departments that it was now able to
oppose a firm front to the assaults of the invader.

Another Armenian noble, Artavasados, son-in-
law of Leo, assumed the purple, and bore the title
of emperor for two years. Of the others who
held this honour, the most distinguished was the
Armenian Leo V. (813-820), who was chosen by
the troops as the only one worthy to ascend the

they were to be delivered to the sword. The refuse of the
people he was commanded not to notice, they being beneath
the anger of the caliph.'

4

throne. It is also a suggestive circumstance that the Byzantine historians have claimed, by way of compliment, for Basil, the founder of a new dynasty, an Armenian descent.

These fragmentary references are sufficient to prove the high character of the Armenian, even during this period of terrible oppression, both for military and civil affairs.

We have thus had a passing glimpse of Armenia during her golden age. We have seen the Scriptures translated into her vernacular and circulated over the land. We have seen religion and literature shedding their united blessings on the people. Again the carnage is renewed, and a race of brave martyrs for their still young faith succeeds to a race of Christian scholars, whose function is to proclaim, expound, and enforce it by research and argument.

In these circumstances the Sword of God is unsheathed on the banks of the Yermuk, and that great victory is won the results of which were to influence so radically the destinies of Armenia, first from the supreme seat of the caliph in Damascus, and thereafter from his throne at Bagdad.

Through the mists of sorrow, of bewildering error in creed and life, Armenia is still holding on her way, not without indications of her high and commanding spirit, until an era is reached which once more carries with it the promise of a return of the long-lost sceptre of her kings to her still imperial hand.

CHAPTER IV.

Dynasty of the Bagratidæ—Rupenian Kingdom of Cilicia
—Relations with the Crusaders — Close of Armenian
Monarchy.

W E ought to premise that the term 'dynasty,'
as applied to the rulers of Armenia
during especially the periods known as
those of the Bagratian and Rupenian rule, is
rather a designation of courtesy than of correct
description. During the long centuries of their
blood-stained annals, they are seldom free from
the oppressive patronage or undisguised tyranny
of the Persian caliph, on the one hand, or the
Greek emperor on the other.

When Ashot, the first of the Bagratian dynasty,
assumed the sceptre of Armenia in 885, the two
most interested powers, the Persian and Greek,
were both favourable to this change, and no doubt
both expected to benefit by it. Under these
auspices a dynasty, the descendants of Sumbat
and Bagarat, and hence of the direct line of
Israel, took possession of the Armenian throne.
During the period of wellnigh two hundred years
of their troubled sway, the history of Armenia

has little other interest save what attaches to a condition of incessant commotion and massacre, arising from the alternating oppressions of Persians and Greeks, as they saw it to be for their advantage to intervene in her affairs. The effusive friendship of both Eastern and Western patrons had begun to visibly cool before a single generation of the new régime had passed away. Issuf, a creature of the Persian caliph, after carrying on hostilities against the Bagratian king, Sumbat I. (the second of the dynasty), seized him and tortured him to death. This miscreant continued his invasions of Armenia in the reign of Sumbat's successor, Ashot II., and spread desolation over the whole land.

Amid these troubles we need not wonder that the condition of the people was not progressive. There does not seem to have been much cultivation of either learning or piety in the pontifical circles, and what feeble Church life there was spent itself in fruitless controversy about the relations of the Armenian and Greek Churches and their doctrinal differences. Perhaps one of the most touching of all the testimonies to the genuine patriotism of the pontiffs of this era is the fact that more than one of them is related to have died of a broken heart for the sorrows of his countrymen.

Owing to the victories of the Byzantine arms, the Saracens were so weakened that the Christians of Armenia raised their banner, and, with the assistance of a division of Greek troops,

'pushed their conquests to the Lake of Van, and
forced the Saracens of Aklat and Betlis not only
to pay tribute, but to allow the cross to be
elevated in their cities higher than the domes of
their mosques.'

The Byzantines and Armenians were not long
destined to fight their battles side by side. In
1022 the Emperor Basil II. compelled the
Armenian king, Johannes Sumbat, to sign a
treaty, ceding at his death the city of Ani, with
the province in which it stood, to the Greeks.
Constantine IX. called upon Gaghik, the last
of the Bagratian kings, to implement this
treaty. On his refusal, Constantine, forming an
alliance with the Saracen Emir of Tovin, laid
siege to Ani. The treachery of the Armenian
chiefs aided the project of the emperor. Gaghik
surrendered, and, receiving a safe conduct, set
out to Constantinople to plead his cause. Meantime the city of Ani was captured by the Byzantine forces (1045). This fatal blow to the Bagratian
monarchy, coming from the hand of a Christian
power, destroyed not only an Armenian dynasty,
but the only barrier to the advances of the
Seljouk Turks. It was therefore in due time
destined to recoil with direst results upon the
head of the assailant.

Following close upon the surrender of Ani, the
Seljouk Turks made repeated incursions into
Armenia. In the third of these incursions they
captured the city of Arzen, 'and massacred in

cold blood 140,000 people ; the remnant they
carried away into captivity.' The native historian
adds that the same cruelties were perpetrated by
this barbarous horde on many other cities of
Armenia. Ani meantime was occupied by 60,000
Greek troops under the command of Camenas,
and these were well pleased to look on with com-
placency at the sufferings of the Armenians.

In 1062, after the death of Togrul, his successor
invaded Armenia and captured Ani.

The energetic reforming labours of the patriarch, Gregory Vikayaser (lover of martyrs), whose
influence extends into the next dynasty, deserve
mention here. Like his great predecessor, the
Apostle of Armenia, whose name he assumed
when he became pontiff, he retired from public
life to end his days in devout seclusion. His
retreat was the Black Mountain, in the regions
of Taurus, where with a few friars he took up his
residence.

We have now reached the close of our brief
survey of the general character of the Bagratian
dynasty. The termination of the chequered
career of the exiled King Gaghik is tragic in
no ordinary degree. Father Chamich gravely
relates how the exiled king visited Marcus, the
Metropolitan of Cæsarea, with a few attendants.
He had heard that Marcus kept a huge dog,
which, to show his contempt, he named Armenian.
Marcus made a show of giving the ex-king a
cordial welcome, and prepared for him a feast

on the evening of his arrival. Gaghik desired his host to call his large dog. The animal, on being brought in, was saluted by his master by the name Armenian. On a given signal, the attendants of Gaghik seized the dog and put him into a large bag. They forthwith threw the metropolitan in beside him, and securely fastened the bag. The dog was then severely beaten, and so, becoming furious, he worried his master to death. Falling into the hands of the Greeks, Gaghik was, in revenge, subjected to the most horrid cruelties, and, after being put to death, his bloody corpse was suspended from the walls of Kigistra, to strike terror into his followers. So perished, says Chamich, Gaghik in the fifty-fifth year of his age. He had been three years in possession of the throne of Armenia, and thirty-five years in exile. The same authority observes : ' A want of prudence removed the crown from the Arsacidæ, and a melancholy want of unanimity caused the downfall of the Bagratians.'

With the overthrow of the Bagratian dynasty, the fortunes of Armenia sunk to a still lower ebb than ever they had done before. A portion of the conquered dominions was seized by the Greeks, while the Turks and Kurds did their best to establish a claim to the rest. At this stage took place a general movement of the Armenians into different provinces of the Turkish Empire, particularly into the regions lying to the west and south of their ancient settlements. Only one or two

native princes continued to maintain their independence. Of these Rupen, related to the Bagratidæ, extended the limits of his dominions, and
his successors advanced to Cilicia and Cappa-
docia, where they established what is known as
the Rupenian kingdom and dynasty.

In the time of Rupen the patriarchate was
weakened by divisions. Instead of one, the
Armenian Church set up four rival pontiffs, but
the general voice was in favour of St. Gregory, to
whose character and reforms we have already
alluded. Around him and successive pontiffs
gathered groups of studious and scholarly men,
whose names and works are still held in honour.
While Rupen and his successors styled themselves kings, it was not until the time of Leo II.
(1198) that the Rupenian kingdom was formally
constituted and recognised by other powers. In
that year, Pope Celestinus III., at the instigation
of the German emperor (Henry VI.), sanctioned
the coronation of Leo, and sent him a magnificent crown by the hand of Conrad, Archbishop of
Moguntia. The emperor sent him at the same
time a splendid standard, having in the middle a
lion rampant, in allusion to his name. This
device was henceforth adopted by the Armenian
kings in lieu of the ancient design of the eagle,
pigeon, and dragon.*

But we have anticipated the grand event
which, in some measure, renders memorable

* Chamich, vol. ii., p. 215.

this era in the history of the Cilician kingdom
of Armenia. This was its temporary connection
with the Crusades. While the new sovereignty
on the west of Asia Minor was struggling
into and for existence first with Greeks, and
then again with Persians, a new enterprise was
rousing to its inmost depths the heart of the
nations of Christian Europe. This was the conception of a grand Crusade, whose object should
be to wrest Palestine and Jerusalem, and Constantinople as well, from the grasp of the infidel.
It was true that at this stage the deliverance of
Constantinople was only prospective, as it was
not yet in the hands of the advancing foe. But
it was easily seen that, with the Turkish camp
already pitched on the eastern shore of the
Bosphorus, this could only be a question of time.
Peter the Hermit, laden with the benediction of
Urban II., and supported by a countless host of
warriors bearing on their breasts or shoulders the
sign of the Red Cross, was now at Constantinople
on the way to deliver Jerusalem. Under the
leadership of Godfrey of Bouillon, this motley
group had made its way to this its first friendly
resting-place and object of succour.

Crossing into Asia Minor, it had found itself in
the horrors of famine and pestilence. The
Armenians both of Eastern and Western Asia
sent abundant supplies, and by their seasonable
services earned the gratitude of the leaders of the
Crusade. The same friendly spirit was shown

also in the case of the second Crusade. On the
capture of Jerusalem in 1099, the leader of the
first Crusade sent the Armenian prince Constantine valuable presents, created him a marquis,
and conferred on him the honour of knighthood.

Amid the turmoil of Saracen conquest, under
Saladin, at Jerusalem (1187), Turkish raids and
consequent capitation taxes, one sees, with some
natural misgiving as to the result, a young girl
of sixteen, the only child of the deceased Leo,
ascend the throne of Armenia. The princess,
however, is beloved from the first by her people,
and though unfortunate in her first husband,
and married against her better judgment to the
second, she is every way worthy of her royal
station. The name of Isabel, the daughter of
Leo II., thus holds an honoured place among
the rulers of Armenia.

But the troubles of the Armenians in Cilicia
and elsewhere were increasing.

The Egyptian sultans, of the race of the Mamelukes, had been making repeated incursions in this
direction, and spreading desolation over the
kingdom of Western Armenia. As a Christian
power, and one which had conspicuously aided in
the enterprise of the Crusades, Armenia seemed
to them a barrier to their scheme of conquest.
The sultan, Shaban, accordingly resolved to
utterly overthrow the dominion of the Rupenian
kings, and to exterminate the nation. He
marched into Cilicia at the head of a powerful

army, took possession of the capital, Sis (1374),
and devastated the whole region, putting the
inhabitants to the sword and demolishing all their
convents, churches, and other buildings.*   Leo VI.
seeing no way of escape, surrendered to the conqueror (1375).   He was put in chains, carried
captive to Egypt, and spent seven years in prison
in Cairo.

Released at last from his captivity, he visited
Jerusalem, Rome, Spain, Paris, and even England.   In vain did he appeal to Charles V. of
France, and Richard II. of England, to embark
on a new Crusade for the recovery of the Holy
Land, and his own restoration to the throne of
Armenia.   He died in Paris, 1393.   The dead
body was decked out in white royal robes, according to the custom of his country, with an
open crown upon his head and a golden sceptre
in his hand.†

From this time Armenia can no longer lay
claim to even the shadow of royalty.   But the
crown of martyrdom still remains, nor did the
national aspirations perish with the extinction
of the monarchy.   We do not here enter into
any discussion of the question as to whether
Armenia has still claims to be regarded as a
nation.   This will appear more manifest as we
continue our narrative.   But we may note even
at this stage that a claim to nationality is not

* Chamich, vol. ii., p. 305.
† Curzon's 'Armenia,' pp. 252, 253.

dependent on any form of civil government, and
is not weakened by any circumstances of bondage
and oppression.

The insignia of a national status are a common
race, a common language, a common religion,
and as the result, common aims and aspirations.

All these characters of nationality distinguish
in a high degree and to the present hour the
Armenian people. For long centuries they have
been deepened under the influences of the national
faith, however degenerate it may have often become, either in form or substance. Nor are
there wanting in these times tokens of a wide-
spread revival of the patriotic spirit.

Following close on the overthrow of the
monarchy by the Mamelukes come the devasta-
tions of Timour, the Tartar sovereign (1403).*

The grim form also of a new tyrant is coming
more and more clearly into view, as he makes his
way through blood and slaughter to his seat on
the throne of the old Greek emperors at Constantinople. Armenian royalty has indeed fallen,
but another and more boastful sovereignty does
not long survive. Twice over the grand old-world
stage is cleared. The actors have come and gone,
and all their scenic surroundings are gone with
them. A new group is crowding on to the stage,
and a new era has opened in the history of the
world.

* Chamich, vol. ii., p. 315.

PART II.

ARMENIA AND THE ARMENIANS UNDER TURKISH MISRULE.—THE PRESENT CRISIS IN ARMENIA.

CHAPTER I.

The Turks and Saracens—Seljouk Turks—Togrul Beg—
Rise of the Ottoman Empire—Fall of Constantinople—
Decline of the Ottoman Empire—Position of Armenia.

WITH the entrance of the Turkish despot upon his blood-stained career, first in Asia Minor and next in Eastern Europe, a new chapter opens, as we have already indicated, in the history of the world. To no portion of his dominions has this change of régime been fraught with more disastrous consequences than to Armenia, where he has indeed proved the very Scourge of God.

To understand, therefore, the tragedy of Armenian history in modern times, as well as what is known as the Eastern Question, as it concerns Armenia, we must be content to deal for a little with the Turkman and his aggressive movements.

The Turks, as this people have been designated from the Middle Ages, are a Scythian race. Their original haunts are to be found in Tartary, and are happily involved in an almost impenetrable cloud of obscurity. In the seventh century after

Christ, this pastoral, roving tribe had overrun and taken possession of the territory—wild and inhospitable as its rude invaders—lying between the Black and the Caspian Seas.

Urged on, like the tiger, by a native thirst for blood and brute force supremacy, they were soon engaged in endless strife with all comers, and with all others who could not keep out of the course of their predatory incursions. The first time we hear of their connection with civilization, and with the reigning power in Constantinople, is when, while still a horde of lawless marauders, scattered over his Eastern dominion, Heraclius, the Greek emperor, succeeded in securing them as his allies in his campaigns against the Persians, about 622.

They shared in the triumph of that great general on his return to his capital on the Bosphorus.

Their next alliance was with the Saracen caliphs, to whom for a time they acted as a body-guard. It was then and afterwards the custom of Oriental sovereigns to depend, in emergencies, on a royal guard of foreigners rather than of their own proper subjects, as more likely, among other reasons, to remain aloof from contending factions, and to espouse on all occasions the quarrel of their paymaster. Hence, we have the Armenian guard (while that people still claimed national independence) and the Varangians at the court of Constantinople, the

Mamelukes in Egypt, and the Janissaries of the Moslem sovereigns.

To the Saracens the Turk was drawn by numerous affinities. As long as the Saracens remained united and devoted to the one purpose of extending the faith of the Prophet, they carried everything before them. In the tenth century they were the most successful warriors in Asia and Europe, and their conquests extended from India in the Far East to the Pillars of Hercules in the Far West.* Yet in this same century the Saracen Empire was dismembered, and the sultans of different countries began to contend for supremacy.

The Saracens, then, while still enveloped in this halo of military glory, not only gratified the warlike propensities of their Scythian ally, but gave him, what he chiefly prized, a Divine sanction for all his nameless barbarities as directed against the infidel. Such, at least, was the Turk's conception or misconception of the provisions of his new-found military creed. In excess of zeal, the neophyte soon surpassed his instructor. It is this picture of a Mohammedan savage which Moore draws with such a masterly hand in the well-known lines :

> ' Hard, heartless chief, unmoved alike
> 'Mid eyes that weep and swords that strike,

---

* Hallam, ' Europe during the Middle Ages,' chapter vi. : ' History of the Greeks and Saracens.'

One of that saintly, murderous brood
To carnage and the Koran given,
Who think through unbelievers' blood
Lies their directest path to heaven ;
One who will pause and kneel unshod
In the warm blood his hand hath poured,
To mutter o'er some text of God
Engraven on his reeking sword ;
Nay, who can coolly mark the line,
The letter of those words Divine,
To which his blade with searching art
Had sunk into his victim's heart.'

From being the mere acolyte of the Saracen, the Turk became himself the superior. In due time he no longer cared to cultivate an alliance in which he was regarded as little else than the ready tool of a power now entering upon the stage of decline. Withdrawing for a time from the position of an ally, the Turkish freebooter found congenial occupation in robbing and slaughtering his hapless neighbours.

At last the motley host found a leader worthy of their cause in Togrul Beg, grandson of Seljouk, a notable chief, who had undergone conversion to the Moslem faith. We need not be too in-quisitive about the antecedents of the new con-vert, but he was a brave soldier and an ardent believer. His family had resided during a brief season in Armenia, from which they had carried away, if nothing else, at least a deep-rooted hatred of the precepts of the Christian faith.

Togrul was not without the graces of his great ancestor Seljouk ; his personal devotion to Islamism was even more conspicuous.

The hour had now come when the Turk must choose for himself a king, and by universal acclaim this honour fell to Togrul. Taken almost directly from the sheepfold, Togrul thus became the first of a dynasty of shepherd-kings. Under such auspices arose the empire of the Seljouk Turk. His accession to the throne was signalized by a formal acceptance by himself and his followers of the creed of Islam as the national religion.

The accession of Togrul dates from 1038, when, having made himself master of Ispahan and Bagdad, he was crowned Sultan of Persia, and received the title of Defender of the Faith and Protector of the Caliph of Bagdad.

In 1052 Togrul began that series of invasions of the Byzantine dominions which was, in the end, to prove so disastrous to the independence of Armenia. The discipline and valour of the Franks and the Verangian guard so impressed him that he retired from his meditated attack on Constantinople without hazarding an engagement.

In 1055 he vindicated his title to the Protector of the Caliph of Bagdad, by espousing successfully his side in a contest for superiority incited by the Caliph of Egypt.

His successor, Alp Arslan, took up the pious scheme of Togrul, and carried devastation and ruin into the ancient kingdom of Armenia. In the

person of Malekshah, the son of Alp Arslan, the
Seljouk dynasty reached the zenith of its power,
and this Sultan was dignified with the title of the
Commander of the Faithful.   The rest of the
history of the dynasty (extending in all from
1038 to 1307) is a record of disunion and gradual
decay.   The final dissolution was hastened by
the irruptions of Genghis Khan, but ere this
time a new master was eagerly pressing forward
his claims to sovereign empire.

In this season of dissolution of the Seljouk and
enfeeblement of the Greek empires, a tribe of nomad
Turks, under their leader Orthogrul, had settled in
the dominions of Aladin, the last of the Sultans
of Iconium.   He had pitched his camp of four
hundred tents on the banks of the Sangar, where
he ruled as a petty independent chief under the
ægis of the expiring Sultan.   To his descendants
belongs the distinction of laying, broad and deep,
the foundations of an empire of which it has
been said that it advanced to greatness more
rapidly than that of Rome, and whose power has
proved more durable than the empire of Alexander.
The honour of this achievement belongs, in the
first place, to the son of Orthogrul, who began
his reign in 1299, and continued to extend and
wisely govern his dominions for the next twenty-
seven years.   The times were favourable for
his ambitious enterprise.   The Seljouk dynasty
was defunct.   The Greek Empire was also ex-
hibiting symptoms of decay, and lay exposed by

the blunders of its rulers to an inroad of the
adversary through the now defenceless passes of
Olympus.   The failure also of the Crusaders
might well suggest dreams of conquest were the
Moslem now in his turn to inaugurate an era of
a *gazi*, or holy war, against the infidels at Constantinople and elsewhere.

In 1299, accordingly, Othman entered Nico-
media, and gave his name to a new race of
Turkish sovereigns, and to what has from this
period been known as the Othman or Ottoman
Empire.   The origin of this new dynasty is computed from the occupation of Brusa as the
capital, an event which took place in the closing
years of the reign of Othman.   Marvellous as
was the success of Othman, it was yet exceeded
by the victories of his son Orkhan, who was
not less great in peace than he was in war.   In
a higher sense than can be said of his father
Othman, Orkhan stands forth as the real founder
of the Ottoman dominion.   ' He is,' says Finlay,
' one of the few legislators who created a nation
and founded an empire by his own legislative
enactments.'

Having gone into some detail as to the rise
of the Ottoman Empire, we shall now pass very
rapidly over our survey of its progress and the
circumstances of its incipient decline.   The institution of the military force of the Janissaries
belongs to the reign of Orkhan.   In the reign
of his successor, Amurath I., the Turk had

crossed the Bosphorus, and Adrianople became the capital of the Ottoman Empire.

Bajazet, his successor, carried his victorious arms from the Euphrates to the Danube. But for his defeat by Timour at Angora, 1402, there is little doubt he would have forestalled the overthrow of the Byzantine Empire by half a century. But the hitherto irrepressible Turkish Sultan was thus arrested in his victorious progress to what seemed boundless European conquest, confined in an iron cage, and carried to Samarcand, where he died in captivity. The Ottoman Empire was now somewhat consolidated under Mahomet I. The aggressive operations were once more resumed under Mahomet's successor, Amurath II., who laid siege to the Greek capital, Constantinople.

In 1453, Mahomet II., the most remarkable, perhaps, of all the sultans, stormed and took the city which was henceforth to be the seat of the Ottoman Empire.

The siege and fall of Constantinople rank among the most imposing events in the transition from ancient to modern history. Constantine XI., the last of the Greek Cæsars, had appealed for help to the Christian powers of Europe—but in vain. The disputes between the Eastern and Western Churches had rendered the prospect of the fall of the former a matter of indifference, if not an object of desire, to the Papal see. The spirit of the Crusades was also largely quenched, and so the citadel of Eastern Christendom, in its hour of supreme need, was left to its own unaided resources. We cannot rehearse the story of the fifty-three days' siege. The forces of the attack and the defence were in sad and suggestive contrast. Around a city, whose Greek population the recent calamities had reduced to about 100,000 souls, with an enfeebled garrison, there gathered the 258,000 soldiers of the Turk, with 320 sail, including all kinds of craft.

The day fixed for the final onslaught, *i.e.*, May 29, 1453, was set apart by the Sultan as a religious festival.

The preceding night witnessed a magnificent illumination of the Moslem camp and ships, transforming the harbour of the Golden Horn, and its vicinity, into a scene of splendour such as, perhaps, had never been witnessed before, or was ever to be witnessed again in the history of Oriental display.

The stated calls to prayer rose upon the still air without, while the pathetic cry of 'Kyrie eleeson' resounded within the doomed city.

The attack commenced in the early morning, and by mid-day Mahomet II. was riding in triumph into his new capital by the gate of St. Romanos. He rode past the dead body of the Greek emperor, buried beneath a heap of the slain. The grand old emperor, whose courage

had supported his people through the horrors of
the siege, had already taken his last Sacrament
in the Church of St. Sophia, and bidden
farewell to his household, ere he went forth
cheerfully to sacrifice his life in defence of the
throne of the Cæsars. But the heroic effort was
in vain. The blow long pending had fallen : the
Roman Empire was no more.

From that period onward, for over two hundred
years, the Turkish warriors were the terror and
amazement of Europe. They conquered and
annexed, to a large extent, the old territories
of Greece and Epirus, also Bulgaria, Servia,
Bosnia, and the countries up to the Danube.
The Ottoman Empire had become in the reign
of Solyman the Magnificent (1520) the most
powerful in the world. In every quarter, east
or west, on even to the Portuguese dominions in
India, he carried forward his conquests. In his
reign, historians agree, the Crescent had at-
tained its utmost altitude.

Before we notice the causes and stages by
which this imposing fabric began to hasten to
its decay, we may here mention some of the
chief causes which are supposed to account for
its rapid rise and progress. These causes were
the superior discipline of the Turkish soldier,
the existence of a standing army, a well-regulated
system of finance, and, lastly, the efficiency of
the artillery. The Turks were the first to

adopt the extensive use of gunpowder, and the use of battering-trains in the siege of fortified places.

Over and above all this we must place their religious fanaticism—the fanaticism of the banner —which so incited and exalted in their heated imagination their native propensities to relent-less spoliation and oppression of the infidel. New influences, however, were now at work, and had been for some half a century, which were destined gradually to undermine the vast superstructure of an alien dominant race at Constantinople. These consisted partly in a series of disasters to the Turkish arms, partly in the steadily ascending power of Russia.

In the reign of Selim II. the tide had fairly turned. The battle of Lepanto, in 1571, gave the first overt signal to Europe of the change in the fortunes of the empire. The prestige of former exploits, however, continued to stand them in good stead until their defeat in 1664 at St. Gothard, by Montecuculi. In 1673 they were again still more signally defeated by Sobieski. The conclusive proof that the Turkish Samson (to adopt the happy phrase of De Quincey) was at last shorn of his strength was not afforded until the great catastrophe of 1683, five years before the English Revolution. In that year an army of 150,000 Turks undertook the siege of Vienna, and a thrill of horror passed over the Christian world.

Then one of those daring feats was undertaken, and accomplished, which justify what otherwise might be denounced as culpable rashness.* The Polish patriot Sobieski, at the head of a hetero-geneous host, less than half 'the number of the enemy, fell upon, defeated, and utterly routed this formidable army.

The victory over the Turks was followed by the treaty of Carlovitz, in 1699, which stripped the Porte of Transylvania, Hungary, the Ukraine, and other provinces. The seat of the Turkish Sultan was now becoming increasingly unsafe and uneasy. The Janissaries, who were wont to constitute a redoubtable bodyguard to a strong ruler in prosperous times, now grew discontented and insubordinate. In short, things had come to such a pass that ' Europe ceased to dread the Turks, and began even to look upon their

* ' Oh for a kindling touch from that pure flame
  Which ministered erewhile to a sacrifice
  Of gratitude beneath Italian skies
  In words like these : Up, voice of song, proclaim
  Thy saintly rapture with celestial aim ;
  For, lo, the imperial city stands released
  From bondage threatened by the embattled East,
  And Christendom respires ; from guilt and shame
  Redeemed, from miserable fear set free,
  By one day's feat, one mighty victory.
  Chant the deliverer's praise in every tongue !
  The Cross shall spread, the Crescent hath waxed dim
  He conquering, as in joyful heaven is sung—
  He conquering through God, and God through him.'
                                              Wordsworth.

existence as a necessary element of the balance
of power among its states.'*

During the period we have been reviewing,
Armenia continued to be the battle-ground
between the Turk and the Persian. From the
time of Selim II. it may be said to have been
incorporated with the Turkish dominion.   In
the wars of Turk and Persian, Armenia was
again and again devastated, and its inhabitants subjected, as so often in later times,
to the cruelty and lust of the soldiers.   A
great calamity befell the Armenians in 1605,
when Shah Abbas overran the country, perpetrated great cruelties on the people, and trans-
ported twelve thousand families to Ispahan, in
Persia.

We do not purpose to follow the course of
the history of the relations of the Turk and the
Armenian into detail, on through the period of
the dispersion of the latter over the Ottoman
Empire, and beyond its bounds, until they come
in recent times into prominence through the
operation of those causes which have given rise
to the Eastern Question, as it respects Armenia
in particular, and especially to those massacres
of our own day, which are the reproach, not
only of the misrule of the Turk, but also of the
civilization of modern Europe.   But in order
that we may approach those more critical, and
let us hope the final, stages of the tragedy, with

* Gordon's ' History of the Greek Revolution.'

a better understanding of its character and malign
design, we must linger a little longer over the
constitution of the Turkish Government, the
relation of Turkish fanaticism to civil and religious
liberty, and, above all, towards the Christian
faith.

CHAPTER II.

Islam as the Religion of the Turk—Youth of Mahomet—
Mahomet at Mecca—Temptations of Mahomet—The
Sword and the Koran — Influence of Islam on the
Character and Government of the Turk—Forced Con-
versions.

WE have already referred to the conversion
of the Turk, and the motives which led
him to embrace the faith of Islam so far
as they bore upon his military career. This change
of religion had also far-reaching results on his
whole character, and particularly as the despotic
ruler of a great empire. This was most conspicuously illustrated in connection with his Christian
subjects. These were found in far greater
numbers under the Moslem dominion of the
Turk than in any other of the earlier conquests
of the followers of the Prophet. In Arabia, Syria,
Egypt, Persia, the subject races, with the excep-
tion of the second of these countries, were
less obnoxious to the Defender of the Faith of
Islam than those of an empire which compre-
hended within its limits the two earliest nations

to embrace the religion of Christ. Of these, for
many obvious reasons, Armenia has been by far
the greatest sufferer.

To understand this state of affairs, we must not
only have some knowledge of the character of the
Turkish barbarian, but of the new religion of
which he is, in many respects, the most remarkable proselyte. We have, therefore, to look a
little more closely at what Islamism really is, and
how it originated.

This will be best done by a slight sketch of its
founder Mahomet, and its exposition in the
Koran.

Little is known of Arabia before the seventh
century. There are floating traditions of Abraham,
Hagar, and Ishmael, associated especially with
Mecca and the Kaaba. On one point all seem
agreed, that there was no record of a rise and
progress—that, in short, the Arabia of the seventh
century did not materially differ from the Arabia
of Abraham and Job. The tribes existed in
separate divisions and subdivisions, defying all
attempts at national union until the appearance
of Mahomet. As to its religious condition, a
deep-rooted system of idolatry, whose headquarters were at Mecca, had existed for untold
ages, and seemed as firmly planted on its soil as
the rugged, bleak mountain ranges which stretched
along its inhospitable interior. The Christian
missionary had been repelled from its borders by
its colonies of hostile Jews, and by an idolatrous

system which had incorporated much of a corrupt Judaism into its national rites. Nor in any case was it easy to evangelize the ever-restless Bedouin, who was no sooner caught than he was sure to find some means of eluding the fixed grasp of the missionary. To Mahomet belongs the distinction of welding these heterogeneous elements into a single mass, and bringing them in his own life-time under the sway of a common faith.

Mahomet was born at Mecca, August 20, 570. His father's name was Abdallah, the son of Abdal Muttalib, the foremost chief of Mecca and guardian of the Kaaba. He belonged to the Koreish tribe, whose chief enjoyed the honour of holding the charge of this central sanctuary of idolatrous pilgrimage.

Mahomet's father died before the birth of his son, and his mother Amina only survived until he was seven years of age. The orphan boy was committed to the tender care of his grandfather, whom he was wont to accompany to the Kaaba, until the death of the latter, which happened at the end of the second year of his custody of the child. After this he was taken in charge by his uncle Abu Talib, who cared for him with parental fondness, as long as he needed such assistance. With him the orphan boy went on a journey to Syria, and was initiated into the mysteries of Arab mercantile life. But the lad was more given to solitary musing than noisy public affairs, and found, perhaps, more congenial occupation as a youthful shepherd tending his sheep on the mountain slopes which overhung his native Mecca. In after-years he was wont to recur lovingly to the memory of these happy, peaceful days, recalling as they did to him the similar avocations of Moses and David, and he would declare to his followers, 'Verily there hath been no prophet raised up who performed not the work of a shepherd.'

The youth of Mahomet was characterized by noble aspirations, by exemplary purity, and by a deeply meditative nature. The sights of Mecca naturally led his acute mind to muse on the folly of idolatrous practices, of which he was a daily witness. Its victims seemed to him, to borrow the metaphor of the Koran, as shipwrecked sailors tossed upon a tempestuous sea, with dark thunder clouds rolling over their heads.

When twenty-five years old, he married Khadija of the same tribe, a noble and wealthy lady, who proved the guardian angel of a long period of his life. Mahomet is described as, at this period, in the flush of youthful manhood, of striking and attractive personal appearance. He was slightly above the middle height, of spare though handsome figure. His head was of the largest calibre, with regal brow. His hair was glossy as a raven's wing, and fell slightly curling over his ears. The eye was dark, flashing, piercing, and the face glowed with animation and intelligence.*

* Sir W. Muir's ' Life of Mahomet,' p. 26.

This commanding presence was a gift which no doubt served the prophet well in his stormy intercourse with his tribesmen at the outset of his career, as well as with others, and at a later stage in his enterprise.

During the early period of his married life, Mahomet was content to enjoy the quiet peace of a happy home. The period, however, of dre ..ns and visions of a higher vocation has begun. He is anxious to assure himself that he has a divine mission to regenerate his people. At length he announces the assurance has been given. He has met with the Angel Gabriel, who brings him his commission, and sends him forth with his message. The supernatural appearance and the message verbally inspired, are minutely set forth.

Returning from the scene of revelation in the cave on Mount Hira, Mahomet becomes for the next ten years an unwearied and vehement preacher of his evangel to the people of Mecca and outlying mission fields. That evangel was little else than the world-wide text of Islam : ' There is no other god but Allah, and Mahomet is the prophet of God.'* It was a direct attack on the ancestral

* ' Nothing,' says De Quincey, ' but the grossest ignorance in Mahomet, nothing but the grossest non-acquaintance with Greek authors on the part of the Arabs, could have created or sustained the delusion current amongst that illiterate people that it was themselves only who rejected Polytheism. Had but one among the personal enemies of Mahomet been acquainted with Greek, there was an end of the new religion in the first moon of its existence. Once open the eyes of the

and all other idolatry. Converts came in slowly, and from the immediate circle of his relatives and friends. First came Khadija; then the circle widened, until, at the close of the first year's labours, he had some forty followers.

As partial success appeared, the Koreish tribe were alarmed; and during the remainder of the prophet's ministry in Mecca, he and his followers were the subject of a fierce persecution. In 621 Khadija died, and almost immediately thereafter took place the Hegira, or flight to Medina. It was preceded by some astute negotiations with the leaders of his adherents in Medina, and by fresh revelations. The faith in his Divine mission was not wont to fail him in even the direst emergencies. On the eve of his flight he was driven, along with his faithful companion Abu-Beker, to seek refuge in a cave near Mecca on the summit of Mount Thaur. It was here his comrade whispered, that they were only two as against a host of the enemy. 'Think not thus, Abu Beker,' was the reply; 'we are two, but God is in the midst—a third.'

Arabs to the fact that the Christians had anticipated them in this great truth of the Divine unity, and Mahometanism could only have ranked as a sub-division of Christianity. Mahomet would have ranked only as a Christian schismatic, such as Nestorius or Marcian at one time, such as Arius or Pelagius at another. In his character of theologian, therefore, Mahomet was simply the most memorable of blunderers, supported in his blunders by the most unlettered of nations.' —De Quincey's Historical Essays ('Greece under the Romans'), pp. 276, 277.

The date of the Hegira is June 20th, 622. We cannot enter into a description of the next ten years, the remaining period of Mahomet's life. During that period Medina was the centre of those forays and battles in which Arabia was at last subdued to Islam. We shall not here trace the course of the successive temptations before which Mahomet fell until at last he gave out that he had received a Divine commission to propagate his religion by the sword.

Students of his life have been struck by the parallel between the temptations of Mahomet and those of the Saviour in the wilderness.

They were, in the case of Christ, temptations to employ supernatural power for the supply of personal wants, and the extension of His dominion by illegitimate means, as well as to convert that spiritual dominion into a coarse and evanescent worldly power. In the case of our Lord the temptation was strengthened by the long cherished desire and expectation of the Jews for a great temporal prince in the person of their Messiah.

The victory of Christ has transmitted to His followers the heritage of a perfect character, and an enduring empire over the hearts and consciences of men.

The failure of Mahomet, under the same ordeal, has bequeathed to the motley throng of his devotees the record of a broken character, which does not improve with years, of a corrupt worldly policy, and a dominion of brute force which has been long sinking to hopeless decay.

The progress of Mahomet's own spiritual life may be best studied in the successive Sowar of the Koran.* They reveal its original sincerity and depth, but they show also to the careful student the not less certain marks of later degeneracy. The Koran grows worse and worse as it advances to completion. Its closing utterances lack the inspiration and high ideal of the earlier sowar. A similar decline appears in the character of Mahomet himself. He exchanges a life of purity for the indulgences of the sensualist. He turns the very Koran itself into an apologist for his vices.

As to the relation of Mahomet to Christianity, he gives it honourable mention in the Koran. Yet all its distinctive doctrines are either ignored or repudiated, such as the divinity of Christ, His atonement and resurrection. This may have been partly due to ignorance, but largely also, there can be no doubt, to an instinctive recoil from its pure and lofty spirit. As Mahomet laid the reins upon the neck of his lusts, and began to wield the

---

* 'The Koran is divided into one hundred and fourteen larger portions of very unequal length, which we call chapters, but the Arabians Sowar, in the singular Sûra, a word rarely used on any other occasion, and properly signifying a row, order, or regular series. . . . It is the same in use and import with the Sûra or Tora of the Jews, who also call the fifty-three sections of the Pentateuch Sedarim, a word of the same signification.'—Sale's Koran, ' Preliminary Discourse,' pp. 40, 41.

sword in the promotion of his cause, his deep hatred of the Christian religion becomes the more apparent, as seen in the mirror of the Koran. The Christian comes, in the mind of the prophet, to rank with the unbeliever. His was the very worst form of infidelity.

It has been said that the Mohammedan religion is considerate in its directions for the treatment of the unbeliever. It does not, it has been pleaded, encourage its followers to kill their enemies, though it fails to restrain the human disposition to do so. Now, the Moslem Turk at least was never much concerned about extracting from the contradictory doctrines of his faith a code of exemplary toleration, supposing such to be found in it. Enough for him that it does not restrain his human, or, rather, inhuman, disposition to massacre, lust and spoliation. ' The sword,' says Mahomet, ' is the key of heaven and hell; a drop of blood shed in the cause of God, a night spent in arms, is of more avail than two months of fasting or prayer : whosoever falls in battle his sins are forgiven ; at the day of judgment his wounds shall be resplendent as vermilion and odoriferous as musk, and the loss of his limbs shall be supplied by the wings of angels and cherubim.'

The question now arises, How does all this bear on the character of the Turk and his government of an empire embracing, as we have seen, so considerable a section of a Christian population ?

We have considered how Islamism affects the character of the Turk as a warrior and conqueror. We have now to inquire how far it helps or hinders him in the nobler task of ruling his conquered dominions. The Mohammedan religion, in its aggressive character, has been compared to a mighty rushing flood, whose tendency, as it flows on, is to purify its waters. But when its inspiring battle-cry dies away into silence, and peace comes to claim its victories, Islamism becomes this same stream gathering in a sluggish pestilent swamp, a reservoir of ever-exhaling corruption.

The process of deterioration was therefore not at first apparent in the rule of the earlier caliphs, Abu Beker, Omar, Othman, and Ali. As an illustration of their simplicity and austerity of life, the dialogue between the Emperor Heraclius and one of the faithful on the entry of Omar into Jerusalem has been often instanced. 'Why,' inquired the emperor, 'does he go in patched clothes, and not richly clad like other princes?' 'Because he cares only for the world to come, and seeks favour in the eyes of God alone.' 'In what kind of palace does he reside?' 'In a house built of mud.' 'Who are his attendants?' 'Beggars and the poor.' 'What tapestry does he sit upon?' 'Justice and equity.' 'What is his throne?' 'Abstinence and true knowledge.' 'What is his treasure?' 'Trust in God.' 'And what his guards?' 'The bravest of the Unitarians.'

The above colloquy could hardly, by any stretch
of imagination, be supposed to describe either the
character or habits of life of the caliphate succession, which has now, for five hundred years
and upwards, revelled amid the delights of the
paradise of the Sultan in Constantinople.

'A rapid degeneracy,' says Hallam, 'enfeebled
the victorious Moslems in their career. . . . Such
is the outline of Saracenic history for three centuries after Mahomet—one age of glorious conquest ; a second of stationary, but rather precarious, greatness ; a third of rapid decline.'

The vices of the Saracen were reproduced and
intensified in Islamism as represented in the
person of the Turk. The Turkish sovereigns also
who ruled at Bagdad were outdone in degeneracy
by their successors, the caliphs of Constantinople.

In regard to government, the Moslem civil law
is based on the Koran, as the civil laws of the
Jews were on those of the Pentateuch. The
author of the Koran was familiar enough with
anarchy and despotism, but ignorant of Roman
jurisprudence, or of the elementary principles of
constitutional government. The idea of religious
toleration will be sought for in vain from such
a source. In its place will be found the injunction
to war to the death against the infidel. The
Moslem is wont to parade his toleration even in
the face of this. This is especially so as regards
the Turkish despot. We admit that more than
one Sultan has played at a game of toleration, and

proved an expert in that exercise. They have formulated the principle in treaties with other governments, as it has suited their convenience, but never attempted seriously to carry it into practice. Despotic as the Sultan is, he is not above the sacred law of the prophet ; by it he rules, and must rule. He must also receive the law as expounded by the Sheik-ul-Islam, the head of the Ulema, or general body of the lawyers and theologians.

This law, as we have said, gives clear directions as to the treatment of the infidel. The non-Moslem, and especially the Christian, is to be treated harshly, beaten and dragged along the ground if he prove unable or unwilling to pay the excessive taxation—a ransom for the right to drag on a miserable and forfeited existence. To enable his oppressor to carry out his purpose—to perpetrate every description of injustice and indignity —-the law forbids the non-Moslem to carry arms. The Christian is thus left defenceless amid his deadliest enemies, armed to the teeth, on every side of him. He must not wear the same colour of clothes, or enter the same bath with a Moslem. The non-Moslem must treat his oppressor with ceremonious respect, in all posible and impossible forms. Any failure in this is punishable with death.

Nor are these oppressions only to be found in the degenerate legislation of the Turk. The following passage from Washington Irving's 'Suc-

cessors of Mahomet ' furnishes a striking illustration of the spirit of Islam *before* it was still
further corrupted by Turkish influence: ' The
articles of surrender (of Jerusalem) were drawn
up in writing by Omar, and served afterwards as a
model for the Moslem leaders in other conquests.
The Christians were to build no new churches in
the surrendered territory. The church doors were
to be set open to travellers, and free egress to be
permitted to Mohammedans by day and night.
The bells should only toll, and not ring, and no
crosses should be erected on the churches, nor
shown publicly in the streets. The Christians
should not teach the Koran to their children, nor
speak openly of their religion, nor attempt to
make proselytes, nor hinder their kinsfolk from
embracing Islam. They should not assume the
Moslem dress, either cap, slippers, or turban, nor
part their hair like Moslems, but should always
be distinguished by girdles. They should not use
the Arabian inscriptions on their signets, nor salute
after the Moslem manner, nor be called by
Moslem surnames. They should rise on the
entrance of a Moslem, and remain standing until
he should be seated. They should entertain every
Moslem traveller three days gratis. They should
sell no wine, bear no arms, and use no saddle in
riding; neither should they have any domestic
who had been in Moslem service. Such were
the degrading conditions imposed upon the proud
city of Jerusalem, once the glory and terror of

the East, by the leader of a host of wandering
Arabs. They were the, conditions generally imposed by the Moslems in their fanatical career of
conquest. Utter scorn and abhorrence of their
religious adversaries formed one of the main pillars
of their faith.'

It appears, then, that even from the outset of
Mohammedan dominion, and when the sword was
just transferred, still warm, from the hand of Abu
Beker, the immediate successor of the prophet to
his intimate friend and faithful follower Omar,
' utter scorn and abhorrence of their religious
adversaries formed one of the main pillars of their
faith.'

This accounts not only for individual oppressive
enactments, but the whole character 'of Moslem
legislation. The administration of the law has
been carried on in the same spirit. And this
applies, of course to all its departments, civil and
religious.

Not only in all the social relations of daily life
do we find this demoniac influence operative. It
shapes the whole ordeal of procedure in the
gravest concerns of life and death, in and around
every Moslem tribunal. No evidence from, the
lips of a Christian, in a court of justice, is considered of any value as against a Mussulman.
Any lying story from the Mussulman is legal
evidence against the Christian. It is a capital
crime to convert a Moslem to the Christian faith.
Yet the self-complacent despot prides himself on
his liberal, large-hearted toleration.

These evils we may expect to see in their worst
form in the person of the ruling Turk.   His relation to Islamism so far explains this.   Possessed
as he is of the qualities which befit the lawless
freebooter—the qualities of courage and enterprise—he could not fail to be fascinated by the
bloodthirsty spirit of Islamism as a military code.
As a system of revealed truth, which it claims to
be, the Turk was mainly interested in the sanction
it gave to his propensities for war and plunder.
Elaborate propositions of principles of government were, alien to one who saw no reason why
his trusty sword should not serve him equally well
for a sceptre as it had done as a weapon of conquest.   On these matters it was not easy to bring
such a neophyte as the Turk up to a respect-
able standard of even Mohammedan orthodoxy.
Though changed by the influences of Islamism in
a very sensible degree, he could hardly be said to
be soundly converted.   Accordingly, when he assumed the position of a ruler. a legislator, or
administrator of the law, he carried with him into
those high functions the instincts and training of
his unregenerate existence.

Our discussion of the relation of Islamism to
the Christian religion could not, we think, be more
fittingly closed than by a reference to the most
recent evidence submitted to the British Parliament on the subject of forced conversions to
Mohammedanism.* That evidence establishes the

* Blue Book, Turkey, No. 5 (1896).   Reports by Vice-
Consul FitzMaurice.

fact beyond all possibility of cavil, in spite of all
that has. been said of Moslem toleration, that
forced conversions to Islam are going on, as the
outcome of a system of organized outrage and
massacre, instigated by the Turkish government.
This is, of course, no new thing in Turkey, but
the scale of magnitude is certainly more appalling
than on most former occasions.

Mr. FitzMaurice's report comes to us with the
authority of an eye and ear witness, and also of one
writing under a strong sense of official responsibility.   He has made searching inquiry, as British
delegate to the Turkish commission at Birejik,
into the state of matters in the vilayet of Aleppo,
and particularly at Birejik, Ourfa, Adiaman,
Severek, Behesni and neighbouring districts.   He
has proved by careful induction of facts that over
6,000 forced conversions of Armenians to Islam
have quite recently taken place within the single
vilayet of Aleppo, and as the outcome of a scheme
of avowed extermination of the infidel.

The story of the massacres and conversions at
Birejik alone is ample proof of the charges involved, and is, besides, as told by the vice-consul,
of such thrilling interest as can never be forgotten
by the most cursory reader.

For two months the Armenian quarter in
Birejik was a scene of Moslem outrage, of daily,
hourly mortal agony under present and prospective
sufferings.   Life had become an ordeal of protracted misery and degradation.   But the worst

still remained to be experienced. On the morning of January 1st, 1896, the trumpet sounded
forth the summons to enter upon the massacre.
The assailants rushed upon the Armenian quarter
of 240 houses. They 'were divided into three
parties, one to break in the doors and walls, the
second to plunder, and the third to massacre all
males above a certain age.' Every house was
pillaged, the churches desecrated and reduced to
ruins. The perpetrators of these crimes boldly
declared that they were acting under the orders
of the Sultan. 'Our Padishah,' they said, 'has
ordered that the Armenians are to be massacred,
and that no Christians are to be left in the
country.'

As the proceedings of this fatal day drew to
a close, the infuriated mob were just about to
break into the houses of one or two Mussulmans
who had sheltered the fugitives, with loud cries
of extermination to the infidel, when an event
occurred which arrested the awful carnage. We
give it in the words of the Vice-Consul : ' Seeing
their desperate determination to break in and
exterminate the Christians, an Armenian woman
ascended to the roof with a white flag, and
declared that they had all become Mussulmans.
The remaining Armenians thereupon repeated the
formula of the Moslem creed, and the mob was
induced to retire on the ground that they were
now attacking their fellow Mussulmans.' Such
is the character of the present conversions to

Islam, which the Sultan recognises as genuine, and cannot see his way to discourage.

In the case of these Armenians, there was no ground for any charge of political agitation. Their only offence was that they were Christians. For such in Turkey, so far as the Sultan dares to touch them, the alternative is a horrible death, or apostasy from their faith.

To renounce the new creed thus imposed upon them is also death by the Sheri Law, as interpreted and executed by the Mussulman. A return to the Christian faith by these Armenians would, therefore, bring about another wholesale massacre. Nay, the very appeal to outside Christian sympathy is a capital offence by the Sheri Law.

Mr. FitzMaurice is well aware that his statements constitute a grave charge against the Ottoman Government, and is duly impressed with the responsibility of embodying them in an official report. On the subject of the forced conversions he thus sums up : ' This conversion question, if not the most serious, is the ugliest feature of recent massacres. It is also the most difficult of remedy, for, though enlightened interpretations of the Mussulman religious and civil law do not sanction such peculiar changes of religion, yet the ignorant masses of the Mussulman population, whose fanaticism has been deeply stirred, and who have now for some time regarded and treated the new converts as Moslems.

would, in case of their reverting to Christianity,
consider them as renegades, and thus punishable
by death, according to the precepts of the Koran.'

Here for the present we must conclude our
survey.

In our episode we have sought to trace some
portions of the career of the man whose spirit
lives and breathes in all Moslem rule. We have
looked upon him in the freshness and purity of
his youth, and as at the close of his ever-
memorable career, he bequeaths to his followers
as his last woeful legacy his Koran and his sword,
the instruments of his temporal greatness, and the
memorials of his betrayal of a heaven-sent trust.

We have witnessed the accession and new-
born zeal of the Turkish proselyte to the faith
of Islam. We have noted the spirit and some
of the maxims which characterize his despotic
rule. We have further shown by bringing our
survey down to the present day that this spirit
and these baleful influences are still at work, and
with as disastrous, if not more disastrous, consequences than ever before within the limits of the
dominions of the Turk. And, in short, we have
seen reason enough to lead us to the settled conviction that from such a source nothing could
be expected but tyrannical oppression, not only
for his Christian subjects, but for all others who
might have the misfortune to own his sway.

CHAPTER III.

Glimpses of Armenian life since the final overthrow of the
Monarchy on to the beginning of the present century—
Persian oppression—Shah Abbas—Armenian Patriarchs
— Roman Catholic influence — Literary revival of the
eighteenth century—Summary.

FROM the overthrow of Leo VI., the last of
the Rupenian dynasty, in 1375, the Armenian Monarchy ceased to exist. From
that time forward even the semblance of civil
autonomy disappeared. Whether, and when, it
is destined to reappear, as the outcome of the
present situation, is one of the questions which
is still awaiting solution. The absorption of
Armenia, now deprived of her kings, first by
Persian and again by Turkish rulers, makes it no
easy matter to trace the course of her chequered
history.

There is no longer a royal centre around which
the drama of the national story may revolve.
The rallying point is now transferred to the
Church of St. Gregory—the institution whose
preservation still, apart from other considerations,

entitles the Armenian to lay claim to national unity.*

The sufferings of the Armenians during this period are largely endured in defence of their ancient Church. The record of these persecutions at the hands of their Persian and Turkish spoilers is without a parallel in the annals of martyrdom. Nowhere have we such a long continued tragedy, such multitudes of slaughtered victims — men, women, and children.

Unable to alienate them from their ancestral faith by the sword of the Prophet, the Turk resorted to those diplomatic devices, sanctioned by his religion, in which he has been long so notoriously an adept.

The Sultan Mahomet II. had, from the first, encouraged Armenian families to settle in Constantinople, and made it the residence of a new Patriarch or head of the Armenian Church. This dignitary (recalling the somewhat similar functionary known in Scottish Church history as the tulchan bishop) was called into existence for merely political and fiscal purposes, and was not owned by the orthodox Armenians as their ecclesiastical head.

The Patriarch of Etchmiadzin still remained

* Chamich, ii., part vii. Father Chamich thus opens this portion of his narrative: 'The order of our history is well connected during the time the Armenians were governed by kings or chiefs. This state being destroyed, we must consider the detail of their actions by the pontificates still permitted to exist, casting an eye at the same time to the contemporary patriarchates of Constantinople.'

the Patriarch of the Church *quoad spiritualia*.
The newly-created Patriarch, however, was the
only legitimate organ of communication between
the Sultan and his tributary Armenian subjects.

He was, for obvious reasons, likely to be the
subservient tool of his Moslem master.

The patriarchal chair, both at Constantinople
and Etchmiadzin, was in the gift of the Sultan,
and was sold to the highest bidder.   The Patriarchs were thus often men of low, sometimes
grossly scandalous, character.   In the same way
lower places in the Church came to be filled with
hirelings.

In these circumstances one of the best of their
number, the Patriarch Melchizedek (1603), made
some effort at reformation.   Groaning, like his
predecessor who still survived, under the ruinous
exactions of the Turks, he took a leading part in
calling in the assistance of the Persian shah, Abbas
the Great.

Abbas did indeed deliver the Armenians for a
time from the oppression of his Turkish rival, but
only to replace it by a still worse oppression of his
own.   The Persian protector of the Armenians
devastated their country, turned loose upon its
defenceless inhabitants his brutal soldiery, who
inflicted on them all the horrors with which we
are now unhappily so familiar, as the accompani-
ment of an Armenian massacre.   The residue of
the people on the scene of these atrocities was
collected on the plain of Ararat, driven as so

many herds of cattle to Persia, and there settled in a suburb of Ispahan.

Twelve thousand Armenian families, and soon after other ten thousand, were thus expatriated amid barbarities such as baffle all description. Among these the massacre of the thousand refugees in the rock cavern overhanging the Valley of Gelard is ever memorable. The women, to avoid a dishonour worse than death, 'rushed to the mouth of the cavern and threw themselves on the rocks below, where they were dashed to destruction.'

Nothing more revolting can well be conceived than the passage by the exiles of the river Arax. As Abbas urged despatch in the transit, crowds of them were huddled indiscriminately into the fragile boats, and these proving insufficient, hundreds of both sexes and all ages, some sick and maimed, were thrown into the river, so that those who could swim might escape to the other side, and those who could not might drown. Many were thus abandoned to their fate, while piteously pleading for help to the last moment of sustaining themselves on the surface of the water.*

On their settlement in Persia, the conqueror treated them with more consideration. He knew their talents for business and enterprise, and hoped from this source to reap no small advantage in the future.

The Armenians henceforth, or such as remained

* Chamich, vol. ii., pp. 353-355.

in their own country, came under the sway of Persian or Turk, according to the fortunes of their frequent conflicts.

In 1655 one of the ablest of the Patriarchs, Philip, Catholicos at Etchmiadzin, was invested with office. In his time Sis yielded the supremacy to the successor of St. Gregory, and the old Church was consolidated and strengthened. This reforming Patriarch, after wisely governing the Church for twenty-two years, according to some accounts, suddenly took ill and died when preaching a sermon on the text, ' Give an account of thy stewardship, for thou mayest be no longer steward.' Father Chamich, who is not wont to mince his statements of the wonderful, and who assures us that Philip more than once performed miracles, does not corroborate the story of the Patriarch's so sudden demise. His account is that the preacher during his sermon had a sudden presentiment of an early death, that a few hours after leaving the pulpit he took ill, and died within eight days.

After his death, and for the next century, the Armenian Church was constantly subjected to persecution. During this period she sunk lower than she had yet done in ignorance and the vicious lives of her priesthood. The lowest point in her degradation is supposed to have been reached in the patriarchate of Lazar—one of the worst who had ever disgraced the throne of St. Gregory. He died in the year 1751.

We need not follow the not very profitable recital of the frequent changes of the patriarchate on to the close of the period under review.

We have said nothing of what may be regarded as missionary enterprise in Armenia, by any outside Church. The Church of Rome continued to make vigorous efforts, through her Jesuit missionaries and others, either to bring the Armenian Church over to herself as a whole, or, if not, to weaken it by schism. In this latter device she succeeded.

As early as the fourteenth century, Peden, a Dominican Father, had drawn away a section to the Roman Catholic see. By-and-by a new liturgy was prepared, and the Latin or Uniat Armenian Church now existed side by side with the old National Armenian Church. The Patriarch of Sis is the spiritual head under the Pope of all the Uniat Armenians in the dominions of either Turkey or Persia.

To this period belongs a movement which bears evidence to the capacity of the Armenians for culture and patriotic enterprise. This is the religious and literary revival which took place in the Uniat Armenian Church in the beginning of the eighteenth century.

An Armenian, named Mechitar, born at Sebaste, in Asia Minor, 1676, having concluded his studies for the priesthood at Etchmiadzin, went to Constantinople. There he fell in with some of the leaders of the Latin Armenian

Church. Convinced that the claims of the Pope were valid, he joined their ranks. He afterwards founded a monkish order, which came in due course to take up its abode at St. Lazarus, in Venice, in 1717.

This society became not less a literary than a religious centre of influence. The monks were united by the common bond of a vow to devote their lives to study and prayer. This Venetian society has republished Armenian classics, as well as produced many original works. Other literary centres are to be found in Vienna, Paris, Moscow, and the schools in Constantinople and Tiflis. These centres, it will be observed, are all outside of Armenia proper, unless we include Tiflis in Georgia as a part of the original Armenian dominion.

These are only a few indications of Armenian life and character in this obscure period in their history. They are, however, sufficient to show the tenacity with which they have clung to their great national institution, and thus, amid incessant changes and dispersions, preserved so largely their unity as a people.

While other nations, such as their tyrants the Turks, accepted the bloodthirsty creed of Islam without a struggle, the Armenians retained their ancient faith, and laid down their lives rather than accept the alien religion. They preferred the ' crown of martyrdom to the white turban of Mohammed.'

At the same time it has appeared, even in our

brief survey, that a process of decadence has been going on in the Old Armenian Church. This has certainly not been arrested by the zealous missionaries of the Romish propaganda. Their influence has been rather to weaken and divide than to unite and strengthen. It is clear that other influences must be brought to bear upon the old Church of St. Gregory, before she returns to her primitive position and function, when her greatest ornament was designated the Illuminator. Her hope of recovery and of noble service in the future lies in her character as a popular institution, around which cluster all the most sacred and enduring associations of long ages of martyrdom.

Her doctrinal errors are rather misconceptions of controversies which wasting persecution allowed her no time sufficiently to master, than direct perversions of the essentials of the faith. Nor does she, like the Church of Rome, mix up the teaching of Scripture with authoritative tradition, or withhold the sacred volume from the perusal of her members. Her present decadent position is suggestively connected with centuries of enjoyment of Turkish toleration. During that time this principle has been in active operation. The Turk has massacred without compunction those who would not embrace his creed. But he has spared the greater portion alive, knowing how useful they might be in raising enormous taxes, and how completely it was in his power to make existence for them a prolonged misery. The Turk

in his magnanimity, has always preferred a slow
to a sudden death.

Meantime, no sooner does the Armenian breathe
a little of the air of genuine liberty, even in the
most questionable companionship, than the native
spirit once more revives with those aspirations and
activities which shed their undying glory on the
eras of St. Gregory, Tiridates, St. Isaac, and
St. Miesrop. The intellectual awakening of the
eighteenth century, though rather outside than
inside the bounds of the mother-Church, is at
once a pleasing memory of the past, and, let us
hope, a happy omen of the future.

CHAPTER IV.

Political situation in Turkey towards the close of the last, and during the first half of the present, century—Degeneracy of the Turk—Russian advances—Peter the Great—Traditional policy of Russia—Reforming Sultans.

THE Turkish Empire had reached the zenith of its power in the reign of Solyman the Magnificent—the contemporary of Charles V., Francis I., and Henry VIII. Since this date the process of decline has been at work. The symptoms of its fatal progress became gradually more apparent, until at length they arrested the attention of Europe in the defeat at Vienna, 1683, which shattered beyond recovery the strength of her land forces, as that of Lepanto had done the strength of her naval power more than a century before. Since the later crisis, Turkey has been sensibly and steadily retrograding as the other Powers, whose very existence she had at one time menaced, have been not less steadily advancing. Some of the causes, internal and external, may well arrest the attention of the student of history.

When wars and conquest were the objects of Turkish ambition, the creed of Islam added the sanction of religion to the grossest indulgence of all his strongest, most cherished native propensities. It had no corresponding inspiration for its rude warrior, when he assumed the rôle of a despotic ruler of his vanquished subjects.

Meantime, in the hands of the non-progressive Turk, even war began to lose something of its terrors for the advancing civilization of Europe. Among the nations of Europe science was re-modelling the old, and devising new and vastly more effective, methods of warfare. It was strengthening their fortresses against the vigorous onslaughts of the barbarian, and providing departments of aggressive assault in new contrivances of artillery, which impressed their astonished antagonists with a sense of the miraculous. Considerable as their own primitive attainments had been in this their only school of education, they did not equip them for these higher studies.

In this state of stagnation or retrogression of the Turkish warrior, medicine was launching its beneficent mission to the camp and the battle-field of his adversary. Considerate attention to the wants of a military force, as to quarters and provision, resulting in a reconstruction of the commissariat, was improving on all hands the efficiency of the soldier. Above all, a tendency to cohesion and patriotism was making its appearance among the quasi-independent provinces where the paramount government was conducted on principles of equity and humanity.

In these circumstances the Turk lost for ever his one golden opportunity, and has now for the last two centuries and upwards been relapsing into a darker Tartarus than that from which he originally sprung. Another cause of the internal decline of Turkish prestige is the quite startling physical degeneracy, the outcome of the moral ulcer of Islamism, as embodied in its sensual character, and so mournfully apparent in Mahomet himself in his closing years at Medina. This is bringing about by the operation of a natural law a rapid decrease of the Turkish race. It has been estimated that within fifty years of the present century the Turkish population of Europe has dwindled from 2,700,000 to 1,150,000. But we turn now to the external influence or influences which have been also at work in hastening the process of dissolution. Chief of these is Russia.

The relation of Turkey to Russia, and the encroachments of the latter upon her dominions and prestige, must therefore for a little engage our attention. Russia, towards the close of the tenth century, so far emerged from her primitive barbarism as to embrace the Christian religion. Her choice of a national faith was conducted on the eclectic principle as the result to some extent of inquiries into existing religious systems. The Greek Church was fixed

upon in preference to other rivals for political
reasons, and reasons personal to the first royal
convert.   The Emperor Vladimir, the first to
embrace the new faith, was about to ally himself to the reigning sovereign at Constantinople
by a marriage with his sister Anne.   One of the
stipulations was his conversion to Christianity.
From this point the supremacy of the Greek
Church was recognised in Russia.

Thus had come into existence a slowly rising
power to the north of Constantinople, which
was yet destined to castigate the Moslem tyrant,
whose boast it was that he had erected the
standard of the Crescent on the ruins of the
Christian dominion of the East.   The vanquished
religion, corrupt as in many respects it had
become, at length reappeared as the fostering,
guiding spirit of the new political power, whose
advances were to shape into form, and to enter
so largely into the solution of, what has now
been so long known as the Eastern Question.

The main steps of the Russian advance are
these : With the accession of Peter the Great
(1689) a new era had commenced in the destiny
and place of Russia among the European
powers.

Before this time Russia had not a single port
on the Baltic ; her only commercial emporium
was at Archangel. But the new Czar at once
set himself to lay the foundations of a great and
lasting empire.   His visit to England in the

reign of William III., his enthusiasm in the ship-building yards and demeanour at Whitehall, excited the curiosity and wonder of the courtly and fashionable circles in London and elsewhere. ' His stately form,' says Macaulay, ' his intellectual forehead, his piercing black eyes, his Tartar nose and mouth, his gracious smile, his frown, black with all the stormy rage and hate of a barbarian tyrant, and, above all, a strange nervous convulsion which sometimes transformed his countenance during a few moments into an object on which it was impossible to look without terror; the immense quantities of meat which he devoured, the pints of brandy which he swallowed, and which it was said he had carefully distilled with his own hands, the fool who jabbered at his feet, the monkey which grinned at the back of his chair, were during some weeks popular topics of conversation.'

In carrying out the programme he had laid down for the formation of a new Russia, Peter the Great took the first aggressive step towards hostilities with the Turkish Empire. In 1696 he gained a decisive victory over the Sultan, Mustapha II., and took from him the port of Azof, thus opening up the Black Sea to the Russian fleet. Three years later Turkey was compelled by the Treaty of Carlowitz to renounce her claims upon Transylvania, and the country between the Danube and the Theiss.

In 1730, in the reign of the Empress Anne, some other triumphs were gained over the Porte. The most formidable, however, of all the Russian foes of Turkey was the sovereign who most fully realized the ideal of Peter the Great, Catherine II. (1762-1774). Not only did she carry on successful wars against the Sultan, but she projected, consistently advocated, and, so far as she could, gave practical effect to a definite scheme to expel the Turk from Europe, and re-establish the Byzantine Empire. This project she prosecuted to her last breath, bequeathing it as a legacy to her successors. Russian aggression therefore steadily continued until, in 1802, the Emperor Alexander annexed Georgia. Further progress was delayed for a time by the meteoric transit of Napoleon across the path of Russian policy. When Napoleon was finally defeated at Waterloo, Russia found herself in possession of a considerable portion of Turkish Armenia. By the peace of Tiflis, in 1813, she gained all the territory west of the Caspian Sea between the Kur and the Arax, Georgia having been already annexed.

The Turks had all along suspected Russia of favouring the insurrection which had lost her Greece in 1822. On the re-enslavement of that noble race, Russia once more moves forward, and the naval victory of Tchesme, in the time of Catherine, with the further concessions of the peace of 1774, are crowned by the decisive engagement at Navarino (1827), and the peace of Adrianople, which at last fully secured the emancipation of the Greeks.

In 1828 war was again declared by Russia against Turkey, and over and above other successes in Europe, the Russian general Paskiewitch took by storm the fortress of Kars, the central point of Turkish Armenia, and finally conquered the whole pachalic of Bagazid as far as the Euphrates. In 1829 Paskiewitch continued his victorious course, and took possession of Erzeroum, the centre of Asiatic Turkey.

Peace was then concluded, and Russia was pleased, for reasons satisfactory to herself, to spare the political existence of her adversary. The chief reason was indeed subsequently stated by a Russian authority to be that the Czar considered he could best advance his own interests by a protectorate over an enfeebled Ottoman Empire. The Sultan then solemnly engaged, as he has so often done, to give religious freedom to all his subjects.

Russia now remained for a season inactive. But the fondly cherished project of Catherine II., if at times somewhat modified, and again and again verbally repudiated, was still, in its spirit, the guiding principle of Russian policy. Turkey must remain, if a power at all, a merely nominal power. To enable Russia to dominate the Black Sea, and establish in due time her coveted protectorate over Turkey, the strong fortress of Sebastopol was erected in the Crimea, and a

powerful Russian fleet now occupied the waters
of the Euxine.

Thus the encroachments of Russia upon Turkey
were part of a settled policy, either for the complete overthrow or the depletion of the Ottoman
prestige.

Always protesting that she wished no more
accessions to her already too vast dominions,
Russia went on extending her boundaries into
Turkey, both in Europe and Asia.*

The desire of Russia to advance to Constantinople has for long ages been more than an open
secret. The Emperor Nicholas, who personally
disclaimed it, declared that you might as soon
arrest the rushing stream in its headlong descent
from the mountain source as arrest the course of
this national sentiment.

An old-world prophecy, engraven centuries ago
on an equestrian statue, foretold the final victory
of the Sclav, and his triumphant entry into
Constantinople.

In Turkey itself the presentiment had been
meantime gathering strength, that unless something were done the Ottoman Empire was hope-
lessly doomed. The old system of *laissez faire*,

* The Russian policy has been thus characterized by
their own historian Karamsin : ' The object and the
character of our military policy has invariably been to seek
to be at peace with everybody, and to make conquests without war ; always keeping ourselves on the defensive, placing
no faith in the friendship of those whose interests do not
accord with our own, and losing no opportunity of injuring
them without breaking our treaties with them.'

it was seen, must be exchanged for one of vigorous action, inspired by the instinct of self-preservation. Such was the state of things in Turkey
towards the close of the last century.

The emergency called forth a series of actively
reforming Sultans who, for a season, did much to
arrest the downward course. Selim III. (1789-
1807) was the first of this new order of Sultans.
He set about internal reforms, favoured commerce
and culture, and made some attempts to reorganize
the military system, or, in other words, to suppress
the Janissaries, and substitute an army modelled
on the civilization of Europe.

This was the proverbial last straw : the Janissaries rose in rebellion and deposed their sovereign. The same fate overtook his successor,
Mustapha II., whose reforms and reign together
extended only over the space of a year.

The ablest and most successful of the reforming Sultans was Mahmoud II. (1808-1839), who
during his long reign, did much to consolidate
the Ottoman Empire and give it a new lease of
existence. Mahmoud abolished the old Turkish
aristocracy, and made the Sultan the *fons et origo*
of all rank and distinction within the empire,
interesting himself in the welfare of all races
and creeds of his people, and was even ostenta-
tiously liberal towards his non-Moslem subjects.

He was at the same time a merciless tyrant,
resorting to the coarse methods of Islam for the
advancement of his most beneficent measures.

8

Blood flowed along his path like water. His destruction of the Janissaries was a display of barbarism only conceivable, as to its grim accessories, by the pagan despot. The hapless victims were driven into an enclosure which could be overlooked by the exulting Sultan and his minions. They were then slaughtered in cold blood, man by man, the Sultan gloating over the scene as some debauched old Roman tyrant may be supposed to have luxuriated over a scene of bloodshed in the amphitheatre.

His attention was in due course distracted from these orgies by the aggressive movements of his Northern foe. His war with Russia cost him Bessarabia and part of Moldavia. The Greek revolution, to which we have already referred, further seriously curtailed his European dominions.

Abdul Mejid (1839-1861) pursued the same general policy, but amid growing opposition. The Crimean war occurred in his reign, and gave rise to a new departure in the treatment of the Eastern Question. So closes this period in the history of Turkey. The degeneracy and misrule of ages had alienated her subjects and laid her open to Russian intrigue and Russian conquest. The advances of Russia, under the banner of the Cross, however unworthily borne, were to some extent a boon, for the time being, to the oppressed Christians of Armenia.

The annexation of Georgi and other Armenian

reforms brought a measure of relief to those Christians who had so long been outraged by the Moslem tyranny of both Persian and Turk.

The reforms at the Divan were late in the day —too late. They were utterly alien to the Moslem spirit, and could not by any possibility be of long continuance. They ran a brief and troubled course towards the close of the last and the first half of this century, but are now as entirely a thing of the past as the early conquests of the Turkish Caliphs of Constantinople, and the prestige itself of the old Ottoman Empire.

CHAPTER V.

New phases of the Armenian Question—Gradual change of policy of the reforming Turk—Protestant influence—American missions—Conflicting verdicts—Political reforms reviewed—Treaty of Adrianople, 1829—Hatti Sherif, 1839 — Protestant Charter, 1850 — Hatti Humayoun in view of prospective demands of the Treaty of Paris—Summary.

THE Turkish reforms may be said to have reached their climax ere the close of the long and vigorous reign of Mahmoud II. (1808-1839).

During this period many abuses were apparently terminated and many beneficial changes introduced into the military and civil affairs of the empire. The Sultan made considerable progress in liberalizing the old despotism, in the promotion of education, industry, commerce, and in certain measures of religious freedom. His son, Abdul Mejid, as we have already seen, continued these reforms, but with far less efficiency and success. He was harassed, as his predecessor had so long been, by the persistent rebellion of his Egyptian viceroy, Mehemet Ali, whom it required the assistance of the English

fleet, under Admiral Stopford and Sir Charles
Napier, to compel to restore the provinces of
Syria to the Sultan. His attention was also distracted by increasing complications with Russia
and their outcome in the Crimean war. His
reforms were opposed with growing obstinacy by
a revival of the old conservative spirit, and
especially as they seemed to aim at religious
toleration for the non-Moslem. The truth was
that the era of reform at Yildiz Palace had
already closed. New forces were coming into
play which were to dissipate the still lingering
reforming fancies of the Sultans, and to throw
them back upon the resources of the old despotic
methods of government. A degenerating race
of sovereigns, the secret slaves of lust and in-
temperance, could not long maintain a policy
based on the confidence of the people, even of
their Moslem subjects.

The religious and political reforms of the
Sultans had never been anything else than merely
precarious and temporary expedients to avert a
visibly approaching doom. Even when the
Grand Turk was in some degree sincere, he was
easily duped by his pashas, who were his agents
in the provinces, and they again, when well dis-
posed, were usually too indolent and careless to
check the lawless ferocity of their subordinates.
This statement is abundantly confirmed by
travellers and others, who now and then, during
this period of ostentatious reformation at the

Divan, got an occasional glimpse behind the scenes of what was ever in reality a woeful tragedy. We shall give a single illustrative instance. It is related at length by the Hon. Robert Curzon, in his ' Armenia,' under the heading ' Case of Artin, Odi Bashi, an Armenian, 1843.'

A charge of theft had been brought against a chamberlain of a khan or inn in the vilayet of Erzeroum. The accused was an Armenian Christian, and the only evidence that of two soldiers, who had confessed to having themselves stolen one half of the goods, the property of a Moslem merchant. They averred that the Armenian, Odi Bashi, had stolen the other half.

The accusation and tortures of the Armenian are described as detailed by the wife of the victim. In order to make him confess the theft, the kiaya ordered him to be put to the torture. A cup of hot brass was put upon his head, two sheep's knuckle-bones were placed upon his temples, and cords were tightened till his eyes nearly came out. As he would not confess, his front-teeth were then drawn one at a time ; pieces of cane were run up under his toe-nails.

Such was the deposition of the wife of the accused, who begged Mr. Curzon to interpose to save her husband from further barbarities. She declared that he slept at home on the night of the robbery.

When the victim was released and examined,

he said he had been tortured, as had been at last admitted by the kiaya, though at first denied. He stated that this was done by the order of his judge, that the bones were put to his temples, some of his teeth were drawn, his nails pierced, his left thigh torn with pincers, he was hung up by the arms by ropes, but the hot cup was not placed upon his head.

Mr. Curzon assures us that on his bringing the matter personally under the notice of the pasha, he found that dignitary deceived by the' false reports of his subordinate, and that he did not know that any tortures had been inflicted. He adds: 'From the above account it appears that much injustice may be carried on by the inferior officers of the Government, which never gets to the ear of the pasha, small officials being notoriously more tyrannical than greater men.'

If such incidents were the warp and woof of everyday life in the provinces when the Turk was at his best as a constitutional ruler, we can form some dim conception of what existence must have been for the hapless Armenian in normal times, when the Turk is at his worst.

A new era, however, did begin to dawn on the Armenian, not as the result of reforms at the Divan, or of his pashas in the provinces, but of reforms from a very different source. This was the influence of Protestant missionary enterprise among the Armenians. The authoritative account of the origin of the chief of these agencies, the American Mission, is to be found in ' Missionary Researches in Armenia,' by Smith and Dwight, 1834. The experiences of the first missionary are related in ' Forty Years in the Turkish Empire: Memorials of the Rev. William Goodell, D.D.,' 1876.

ı While there are other agencies at work, the American missionaries easily take a foremost place. They have proved the pioneers of civilization in Asiatic Turkey. Nothing has tempted them to desert the post of duty in the times of greatest trial and peril. Their sympathy with the suffering, their wise counsel, their Christian heroism, are well known and beyond all praise. Their labours are carried on under the control of the American Congregational and Presbyterian Boards. The Congregational is the stronger of the two wings of this salvation army, and at the present rudimentary stage it would be no easy matter to organize a Church upon Presbyterian lines. The centres of presbyteries, synods, and assemblies would present geographical difficulties not experienced in the working of Congregationalism. The direct results are in the highest degree creditable to the missionaries, especially when the opposition they have had to encounter is taken into account. The indirect results are the awakening of a spirit of inquiry, and the inauguration of a forward movement among the Armenians chiefly, and in some degree among others who have come under the influence of the missionaries.

The best proof of the elevating influence of their educational work is found in the new-born zeal of the present Sultan for the establishment of schools, on behalf of his Moslem subjects, and his hostility to the missionary institutions.

That the American missionary has entered Armenia as the harbinger of an era of progress for its down-trodden people is now pretty generally admitted. We may certainly trace to this source all the more recent progressive movements of that community.

The religious revival has, as usual, been followed by a revival of the spirit of individual and political freedom.

The Turk cannot relish these tendencies, and yet the present Sultan has been forced to own that the missionaries are free from any sinister political designs.

There have been critics of Protestant missions, and therefore, of course, American missions, who have not been so equitable in their judgment as the Sultan. They have spoken of them as having no fixed creed, as so many warring sects, whose chief achievement has been to produce a barbarous translation of the Scriptures, which is the subject of ridicule and contempt to all cultured Armenians.

These, however, are now obsolete verdicts. There has been a steadily-growing appreciation of the influence for good of the American missions.

Quite recently a strong light has been cast on this subject in a pathetic letter from Armenia, published by Sir William Muir, and entitled ' Armenia's Farewell ' (January, 1896).

Sir W. Muir says, by way of introduction to this ' genuine wail of the horror-stricken people,' that since the fourteenth century, when Leo VI., the last of the Armenian kings, was taken captive and the dynasty overthrown, there has been no such attempt as is now being made to exterminate the Armenian race or convert them to Islam. The following is an extract containing the closing portion of the above-mentioned letter :

' To the Christians of America.

' Although we have cherished strong prejudices against your mission work among us, recent events have proved that our Protestant brethren are with us, and have shared fully our anxieties and our perils. This has brought us very near to you, and, if there were any future for us, we should prize your Christian love and fellowship as never before; but we are marked for destruction, and can only bid you farewell. You have laboured to promote among us the peace and prosperity of the Gospel. It is not your fault that one result of your teaching and example has been to excite our masters against us. You, at least, know the situation too well to believe for a moment that we are being punished for political sins. You cannot fail to see that, so far as we have been the occasion of the bloody massacres which have come upon us, our crime in the eyes of the Turk has been that we have so fully accepted, and so far adopted, the Christian civilization of the West. You are quite aware that the Turkish Government dreads and dislikes nothing so much as the ideas of progress which you have brought us. Behold the missions which you have planted and maintained among us at the cost of many millions of dollars, and hundreds of precious lives. They are in ruins; and not only this, the Turk is planning to rid himself of the missionaries by leaving nobody among and for whom to work. A short year ago, and nobody could have believed that at the end of this nineteenth century—a century characterized by the collapse of Islam and the advance of Christianity to a position of unquestioned supremacy in the government of the world —a Christian people could, on account of their loyalty to Christian civilization, and under the very eyes of Christendom, be exterminated by a Mohammedan power. Yet just this fearful tragedy is being consummated to-day. Already hundreds of Armenian villages have been wiped out, and in the larger towns and cities our people have been decimated, plundered, crushed. We see no signs of relenting on the part of our destroyers, and no hand is reached out to rescue us. We have only to say farewell to any who have loved and cared for us, and prepare ourselves for the butcher's knife, honoured in closing

and sealing our national history of forty centuries
with our blood.'

We turn now for a little to trace the general
course of those political reforms, emanating in the
first place, as we have already stated, from the
constitutional Sultans, and which, no doubt contrary to the design of their authors, were as the
letting out of the waters of the rising tide, which
threatens at no distant date to submerge the
throne of the Turkish Empire.

First, we have the Russian autocrat suggesting
a larger measure of freedom to his co-religionists,
especially the members of the Greek rather than
the Armenian Church.   This was promised by
Mahmoud II. (the greatest of the reforming
Sultans) in terms of the Treaty of Adrianople,
1829.

The characteristic diplomatic system of profuse royal promises embodied in magniloquent
firmans was now a recognised policy of Ottoman
rule.

Abdul Mejid, Mahmoud's son and successor,
issued, in 1839, an imperial rescript, the Hatti
Sherif, engaging to protect the life and property of
all his subjects, whatever their race or religion.
In 1844 he gave a solemn pledge that no apostate
from Islamism, who had formerly been a Christian, should be put to death.   Still further, this
same Sultan granted in 1850 what is known as
the Protestant Charter.   The Charter concedes

the fullest measure of religious freedom. Lastly, Abdul Mejid, just before the Treaty of Paris had been completed, in 1856, issued the imperial edict, the Hatti Humayoun, which guarantees perfect equality of civil rights to all the subjects of the Porte, as also the largest conceivable degree of toleration, in these words: 'As all forms of religion are, and shall be, freely professed in my dominions, no subject of my empire shall be hindered in the exercise of the religion that he professes, nor shall he in any way be annoyed on this account.'

These fair promises were none of them kept. The same iron yoke of oppression rested on the necks of the Christian populations of the empire, and especially the Asiatic portion, though this has been the last to arouse the practical sympathy of Europe.

The burden of oppression fell chiefly on Christian Armenia. While Georgia afforded a safe civil asylum to the Armenians under Russian rule, and Persia even was a place of refuge, Turkish Armenia was only entering on a new and sure heritage of indescribable suffering and degradation. Such was the state of things when Russia stepped in with her ultimatum claiming a protectorate over the Christian subjects of the Ottoman Empire, and this as the fulfilment of a pledge already given to the Czar.

We have thus seen that the policy of the Turkish Sultans gradually reverted to the ideal of the old

despotism. Any sincerity of purpose which may
have existed when reform seemed the sheet-
anchor of political stability had gradually given
way to the native habit of mind. Meantime, in
this way, an impulse had been given to a new
state of things. The spirit of reform was now
astir.

We have glanced at the fostering influence of
the American missionaries. The stage of mis-
representation, we have said, is past, and the
hope may well be indulged that this agency, with
its Robert College at Constantinople, and other
educational institutions sending forth its pioneers
in the Crusade of the nineteenth century, has yet
many triumphs before it in the prospective re-
generation of Armenia and the other Asiatic
portions of the Turkish Empire.

We have also noted retrospectively, and up to
the new departure in 1856, the trend of political
reform in Turkey under Russian pressure, and in
the shape of certain pledges given with truly
Oriental profusion by the reigning Sultan. Connected with the Russian idea of world-wide
conquest, we ought to add, is that of the co-ordi-
nate extension of the influence of the Greek
Church.

The Greek Church aspires, as far as possible,
to advance *pari passu* with these conquests. That
Church, long at variance with the Latin on
questions of relative superiority, was at last
formally excommunicated and anathematized ' by

the Roman See, on account of having embraced the heresy that the Holy Spirit proceeds only from the Father, and not also from the Son.'

The 'Filioque' Shibboleth, it has been well said, has ever since divided the Eastern from the Western Churches, even more completely than the Bosphorus divides Asia from Europe.

The alliance between the Church and State in Russia is of the closest kind. The Erastian problem was promptly solved one day by the sudden entrance of Peter the Great into the conclave of bishops, about to elect a new Patriarch, with the announcement that he himself was henceforth to be their Patriarch. With such an authority, argument was out of the question, and from this time forward the Russian Czar has been recognised as the Head of the Greek Church.

There can be no doubt that the strong feeling of jealousy between the Greek and Latin Churches, giving rise to the petty squabble about the custody of the keys of certain holy places in and around Jerusalem, and ending in unpardonable humiliation for the Czar, was the real cause which precipitated the Crimean war, from which we date a new and important phase in the relations of the Powers of Europe to Turkish misrule in both the Eastern and Western divisions of her empire.

CHAPTER VI.

European concert and its relation to Turkey—Treaty of Paris, 1856 — Turkish diplomacy— Young Armenia— National Constitution (1862) and National Commission (1871) — Situation before the Treaty of San Stefano— Cyprus Convention and Treaty of Berlin (1878)—Sixty-first and Sixty-second Articles—Peace with Honour—Summary.

WITH the events which ushered in the Congress and Treaty of Paris was inaugurated on a European scale the subsequent continuous policy of the Christian Powers towards the Turkish Empire.

Three centuries or so before this date the dream, it has been said, of every statesman in Europe was the expulsion of the Turk from Constantinople, and the emancipation of Christian Europe from the oppression of the infidel. At the period to which we now refer, the close of the Crimean War, we find the six great Powers of Europe resorting to every expedient of diplomacy, not stopping short of remedial measures of coercion to retain the Turk on the throne which he had so long disgraced, and which was now tottering visibly to its fall.

The reason of this change of policy is worthy of some attention, and brings us back again to note the aggressive movements of that Power which had for so long been fraught with the kismet of the foredoomed Moslem. That Power, of course, is Russia.

Ever since the brilliant victories of Catherine II. a feeling had been gaining strength in the cabinets of Europe that the sword of the Czar was at the throat of the Sultan, and that the fatal stroke would fall at the earliest moment when it could be delivered with impunity. The instinct of self-preservation, in a lesser degree that of sympathy with the distress of the conscious victim, and above all a regard for the public weal of Europe, combined to bring into prominence the doctrine of political expediency, known as 'the balance of power.'

Should Russia plant the banner of the Cross on the Mosque of St. Sophia, this already overshadowing Colossus would, it was believed, endanger the liberties of Europe. Great Britain in particular saw in this possible event a menace to her prestige in the East. Other European Powers nearer Constantinople saw cause for uneasiness in the prospect of the new régime. The vision of a motley throng of Ural Cossacks mustering on the shores of the Bosphorus for an incursion into the plains of Europe had terrors enough in it to disturb the most sober imagination. Even in England it was long remembered

9

that one of the chiefs of these Frankensteins of
Russian power had, shortly after the battle of
Waterloo, nudged Field-Marshal Blücher as they
passed along the London streets, and exclaimed:
' What a city for to shack !'

The theory, therefore, was that the maintenance of the Turkish despot was necessary
to preserve the balance of power, and so far
guarantee the peace of the nations of Europe.
To this strange theory Turkey has since then
owed, not only its existence as an empire, but
a recognised place in the concert of Europe,
as well as all the power she has since so grossly
abused in the misrule and massacre of her non-
Moslem subjects.

But to return to our survey of the course of
events. We shall now see how this theory has
been elevated into an international principle, and
carried into practice in the provisions of the treaty
which followed the Crimean War, and the issue
of the Hatti Humayoun, i.e., the Treaty of Paris.

The Crimean War arose ostensibly from the rejection by the Sultan Abdul Mejid of the ultimatum
presented by Prince Menschikoff on behalf of
Russia. In it the Czar claimed a virtual protectorate over the Christian subjects of the Sublime
Porte, or three-fourths of the population of
Turkey. This was not advanced by him as a new
claim, but as a right which had been conceded in
terms of the treaty of 1744. This construction of
the treaty was denied by Turkey and her allies.

More strictly, the claim had reference to the members of the Greek Church, yet could be so construed as to embrace the whole Christian population.

The European Powers supported the Sultan in his rejection of the Russian ultimatum, and England and France sent their allied forces to the Crimea. On the conclusion of the war, and a new firman from the Sultan (Hatti Humayoun) granting religious freedom to his subjects, the Treaty of Paris, incorporating this firman, was drawn up as an international guarantee for the execution of these reforms. The Crimean War having been undertaken to arrest the steady encroachments of Russia, and to secure new guarantees for the independence of the Ottoman Empire, one provision of the treaty was that Russia should withdraw her claim to a protectorate over the Christian subjects of the Sultan.

The responsibility of protecting the Christians of Turkey from Moslem outrage thus devolved, by their own act, upon the European Powers. Russia was thrust out of Turkey, and the Sultan no longer needed to dread her control. Not only was Russia deprived of some of her land conquests over Turkish territory, but her naval strength on the Black Sea was destroyed, and she was bound by the treaty not to restore it.

The text of Article IX. of the Treaty of Paris, which is designed to remove the pretext for

Russian interference, runs thus: 'His Imperial Majesty the Sultan having, in his constant solicitude for the welfare of his subjects, issued a firman which, while ameliorating their condition without distinction of religion or of race, records his generous intentions towards the Christian population of his empire, and wishing to give a further proof of his sentiments in this respect, has resolved to communicate to the contracting parties the said firman emanating spontaneously from his sovereign will. The contracting Powers recognise the high value of this communication. It is clearly understood that it cannot in any case give to the said Powers the right to interfere, either collectively or separately, in the relations of his Majesty the Sultan with his subjects, nor in the internal administration of his empire.'

The remedy for all complaints in the government of Turkey, when they can be no longer ignored, is an imperial Hatti promising immediate and superabundant redress, and granting all imaginable reforms. These engagements being made under physical constraint, and only to the infidel, are not seriously meant, and remain, so far as the spontaneous action of the sovereign will is concerned, a dead letter. This has been notoriously the case as to the engagements undertaken through the treaty we are now considering.

There are, it is said, three phases of Turkish diplomacy. There is first the open defiance of the Powers insisting on faithful performance of

stipulated compacts, when this can be resorted
to with impunity. When this attitude cannot be
assumed, there is the second phase, which is an
assurance of compliance with the demand, given
with all the solemnity of a devout Moslem. No
semblance even of performance is ever attempted.
In the third and most desperate stage, from the
Moslem point of view, along with the solemn
pledge there is some deceptive appearance of
performance.

So far was Turkey from intending to carry out
the reforms of the Treaty of Paris that from that
time there commences a new era of oppression.
In Armenia, however, a forward movement
seemed to have begun. The idea of religious
freedom came upon the Armenians as an inspiration. Their religion, for which they had endured
so many persecutions, was the one thing the
Turk had not taken or could not take from them.
Their hopes of a future centred in guarding this
sacred trust. It was the Palladium of their
beleaguered land, and so long as it remained with
them they were safe. The promised liberty now
guaranteed by the European concert awakened a
new life inside and around the long-desolated
shrines of their martyred forefathers.

The Turk, lynx-eyed as to the detection of any
movement of emancipation, and resolved to crush
it at the outset, soon took note of the new birth
of what we may name the party of Young
Armenia.

This party was in earnest about reform, and reform on such constitutional lines as were now opened up by the Hatti Humayoun, and the Paris Treaty, which, by placing it as the first of its articles, gave it the emphatic sanction of the Powers of Europe. The party, in striving to have these reforms carried out, was acting on strictly constitutional lines, and in a spirit of loyalty to the Ottoman Government. Nothing is more discreditable to the Turk than his hypocritical attitude towards these revived aspirations of his Armenian subjects.

While anxiously waiting for some indication of the practical results of the treaty pledges, they discovered that the Sultan under the sanction of the treaty provision, was initiating his reforms by an alleged necessary restriction of such limited independence as had originated and been fostered in the bosom of the mother-Church.

They not only had the courage to protest against this insidious attack on their liberties, but to insist on some personal share in the administration of their affairs.

The Sultan, 'in his constant solicitude for the welfare of his subjects,' on hearing a representation of the grievances complained of, met the advances of Young Armenia by the magnanimous offer of a bran-new National Armenian Constitution (1862).

This paper constitution is a complicated piece of radical legislation, made up of 150 provisions, which, if really brought into operation, would

have converted Armenia into a political paradise.
We need not enumerate its lofty sentiments, its
educational and religious reforms, its profuse and
cordial encomiums of the Turkish ruler. Never
was there a more imposing catalogue of high-
sounding promises.

A full account of this wonderful Magna Charta
of Armenian freedom is given by M. G. Rolin
Jæquemyns, in his articles in the *International
Law Review* (1888-9), to which we refer the
reader.

Five years passed, and as no real advance had
been made to serious action, it was resolved by
the National Assembly, which had now a nominal
existence, to appoint a National Commission to
inquire into unredressed grievances and to suggest
remedies. This Commission was appointed in
1871, under the presidency of the Patriarch of
Constantinople. Almost the only good service
the Armenian Constitution had done was to provide a channel through which the Sultan might be
approached by the Armenians, with their legitimate complaints and appeals for reform. These
cries of distress were now being heard from all
quarters, and even if they fell, as they did, on
deaf ears in the kiosk of the Sultan, there were
others prepared to listen. The Patriarch of Constantinople drew up the first report of the National
Commission (with its black list of grievances of
oppression in taxation, forced conversions of
women and minors to Islamism, Turkish and

Kurdish outrages on women and children), submitted it to the Grand Vizier, Mahmoud-Nedim-
Pasha, in 1872, and again on several occasions to
his successors.

After four years' hopeless waiting for a response,
a second report was submitted, calling attention
to new abuses. These arose from the brutal lust of
the Turkish officials, and the iniquitous proceedings of the law-courts in which such cases were
tried, and where the decision invariably was on the
side of the Moslem and his accomplices. The
report enters into minute details of instances, as
the Sultan had declared that no attention could be
paid to general charges. The list of lands wrong-
fully appropriated by their spoilers from the
Armenians, with the names of the culprits, covers
ten pages of the report.

It would be impossible within our narrow
limits to analyze the contents of this terrible indictment of Turkish misrule. During all these
outrages, it must be remembered that Moslem
Sacred Law forbids to the infidel the use of
arms even in self-defence, while it fully equips
every chance marauder who can be pressed into
the service of their oppression. Even to some of
our English statesmen this policy has seemed
defensible. When the other Powers of Europe,
in the Berlin Memorandum, proposed to demand
the fulfilment of the Sultan's treaty engagement
to permit the Christians the use of arms, Lord
Derby opposed them on the singular pretext that,

should the Christians be armed, 'a collision would be inevitable'! When the other Powers pressed his obligation on the Sultan, he, of course, had no difficulty in evading his promise by securing a decision from the Sheik-ul-Islam (the supreme authority in the Sacred Law), in consultation with the Ulema of Constantinople, that such a concession was *ultra vires* even of the Sultan, who cannot alter a single iota of the Sacred Law.   In short, the first obstacle to all Governmental reforms in Turkey is just this Sacred Law.   The Turkish Government is a Moslem theocracy, and cannot be altered in principle, being already a final expression of the will of Allah.   The Koran, with the traditions founded on it, rules supreme.   Its spirit is not only hostility, but the most degrading bondage or death to the infidel.

Canon MacColl, in his 'England's Responsibility towards Armenia' (1895),* mentions four outstanding grievances of this rule of Islam or theocratic system, all of which mean untold sorrow and humiliation to the Armenian, above any other subject of Turkey.   These grievances are, the exclusion from rights of citizenship, the rejection of Christian evidence in law-courts as against a Mohammedan, the prohibition above referred to, of arms to a Christian, and what is known as the law of the Hospitality Tax.

* Every reader will endorse the judgment of the Duke of Westminster on this pamphlet, that a more authoritative or clearer demonstration of Turkish misrule could hardly be drawn up.

As regards the stringency of the law respecting
Christian evidence, the Rev. Dr. Wright, head of
the Irish Presbyterian Mission at Damascus,
says : ' I was present in the Supreme Court of
Justice at Damascus when the evidence of her
Britannic Majesty's Consul was refused by the
judge, because he was a Christian, and the
evidence of his Moslem stable-boy taken instead.'

Commenting on the Hospitality Tax, according
to which every Christian subject of the Sultan is
bound to provide three days' gratuitous hospitality
for every Mohammedan traveller who chooses to
demand it, Canon MacColl gives the following
extract from a description of Mr. Nassau Senior
(1860). It is not so much a picture of any
scene of the periodically recurring massacres, as
of the everyday life of the Christian rayah under
the tyranny of this one sacred law of hospitality.

' Besides the wholesale robbery of the great
Turks, there is,' he says, ' the petty oppression of
the little Turks. One of them, with his belt full
of pistols, walks up to a rayah's house. He calls
out the master, who perhaps is the headman of
the village, and bids him hold his horse. He
walks in, sits down, and makes the women light
his pipe. The girls all run away and hide in the
outhouses, or among the neighbours. When he
has finished his pipe, he asks for a fowl. He is
told there is none. A few blows bring one out ;
a few more bread and wine. What is the source
of this insolence ? That he is armed, and that he

is the only person in the village who is. If the rayahs were armed or the Turks were disarmed, there would be none of this petty oppression.'

These oppressions are not confined to this or that province. The Central Government from time to time issues an irade condemning glaring cases, but little or any notice is taken or meant to be taken by the provincial pasha. And so the tragedy, treaty or no treaty, goes on, and Young Armenia is destined to see its dream of a brightening future changing into a horrible nightmare.

As regards the cause of reform generally, not only in Armenia, but throughout the Turkish Empire, this was from the first enfeebled by the omission from the Treaty of Paris of the substance of the Hatti Humayoun, as a formal provision, and the substitution in its place of the notification of the good intentions of the Sultan, 'emanating spontaneously from his own sovereign will.' This diplomatic phraseology was adopted on the representation of the chief Turkish plenipotentiary, Ali Pasha, as a necessary avowal to preserve the dignity and to secure the success of the reforming measures of the Sultan. Ali Pasha was at that time Grand Vizier of Turkey, and amid the many changes of the vizierate of the next fifteen years of his life, his influence was thrown into the scale of keeping up an appearance of reform, and a reality of incessant parade of the independence of the Sultan.

The European Powers, crediting, it would seem,

the Turkish Government with a measure of good faith, were content to be merely onlookers as the terrible tragedy proceeded.

Meantime the successor of Ali Pasha, as the real guide of Turkish policy—Mahmoud Nedim Pasha (to whom we have already said the Patriarch of Constantinople submitted the first report of the Armenian Commission), threw off the too transparent mask. He adopted the popular rallying cry of 'Turkey for the Turks,' and at the same time the principle that Western measures of reform were unfitted for the habits of an Oriental empire. There was henceforth no pretence to adapt Turkish administration to European notions of justice and humanity. This stubborn attitude made the reopening of the Eastern Question merely a matter of time and a fitting opportunity.

The occasion was given (July, 1875) in the insurrection of Herzegovina. The chief grievance was over-taxation and oppression, in defiance of the Hatti Humayoun. The revolt was one of those occurrences in the history of an oppressed people which prove so disastrous in failure, yet when successful raise their instigators to the rank of heroes and patriots. This movement led the European Powers at last to take some overt united action, and the presentation of the Andrassy note—demanding certain reforms in Bosnia and Herzegovina — was the practical outcome. The astute Nedim Pasha tried the proverbial ten tricks of the fox to avert the issue, but only with reynard's proverbial success. A new Constitution was proclaimed, 1876, exceeding in its radical character anything contemplated by the guaranteeing Powers. But Europe had enough of Turkish constitutions.

Such was the position of affairs when Russia again interposed, and offered to secure, by force of arms, the due performance by the Sultan of his treaty obligations. The Bulgarian massacres were by this time arresting the attention of Europe, France had been crippled by the Franco-German War, Germany and Austria were in alliance with the Czar, Italy was also friendly, even England was lukewarm—all, in short, were prepared to stand aside and give Russia, so far, a free hand in the settlement of the now reopened question.

We cannot give details of the Turco-Russian war which followed, the brave endurance of General Gourko and his forces, the desperate resistance of Osman Pasha, until, by the fall of Plevna, the struggle was virtually ended.

The Turkish Government had taken no notice of any of its defeats in the official press, and had considerable difficulty in climbing down so far as to give any indication of a desire for peace.

But the victorious Russian army was pressing on to San Stefano, only six miles from Constantinople, and the serious nature of the position could no longer be dissembled. One sure precursor of the commencement of pacific negotiations was noted in the change of tone of reference to Russia.

The official press saw fit to warn the people not to speak of Russia as the Bear of the North, as such language was disrespectful, and contrary to the rules of courtesy in vogue among civilized nations.

The war was finally concluded under the shadow of Constantinople by the Treaty of San Stefano (March, 1878).

At the date of the Treaty of San Stefano, Russia was occupying, by right of conquest, a portion of Turkish Armenia. She had taken possession of Kars and Erzeroum. Not only had a number of Armenian officers, subjects of Russia, fought bravely in the ranks, but the Commander-in-Chief of the Russian Army of Asia was an Armenian, Loris Melikoff.

We are therefore prepared to learn that to this treaty belongs the distinction of being the first to mention the name of Armenia.

The protocol and agreement for an armistice, signed at Adrianople immediately previous to the San Stefano Treaty, makes no mention of the Armenians. But the energetic patriarch, Nerces, got the omission rectified.

In the San Stefano Treaty two facts were recognised—the necessity of local reforms and of the safe-guarding of the Armenians from the outbreaks of the Kurds and Circassians. The treaty

was a Turco-Russian agreement, and its sixteenth
Article, forming the basis of the sixty-first Article
of the Berlin Treaty, ran thus :

'As the evacuation by the Russian troops of
the territory which they occupy in Armenia, and
which is to be restored to Turkey, might give rise
to conflicts and complications detrimental to the
maintenance of good relations between the two
countries, the Sublime Porte engages to carry into
effect, without further delay, the improvements
and reforms demanded by local requirements in
the provinces inhabited by the Armenians, and to
guarantee their security from Kurds and Circassians.'

Nowhere did the terms of the Treaty of
San Stefano arouse more jealousy than in this
country. The Treaty had been, it was said, in
a memorandum issued by the Porte, extorted
from Turkey by the 'permanent pressure' of
Russia.

It was argued that it was opposed to the
governing principle of the Treaty of Paris, which
placed the affairs of Turkey under European and
not any individual supervision.

Then followed much talk of British interests
and British influence, the dispatch of the
fleet to Besika Bay, and preparations for the
coming conflict if we did not get our own
way.

In these circumstances the final arrangements
for the Berlin Congress were carried through,

and Lord Beaconsfield and Lord Salisbury were
sent as our plenipotentiaries to the Congress.
By a memorandum previously drawn up and
signed at London (May, 1878) by the Marquis
of Salisbury and Count Schouvaloff, it had been
agreed that : 'The promises respecting Armenia
stipulated in the preliminary Treaty of San
Stefano must not be made exclusively to Russia,
but to England also.'

The task of the Berlin Congress was therefore
thus described by its President, Prince Bismarck:
'It is for the purpose of submitting the work of
San Stefano to the signatory Powers of the
treaties of 1856 and 1871 for free discussion that
we have met.'

The Congress was, however, accompanied by
a transaction of another kind which it required
all the resources of the Jingoes of the day to
explain, and even plausibly defend. This was
the private treaty between England and Turkey,
known as the Anglo-Turkish or Cyprus Convention. Its first Article runs thus: 'His Imperial
Majesty, the Sultan, promises to England to
introduce necessary reforms, to be agreed upon
later between the two Powers, into the government and for the protection of the Christian and
other subjects of the Porte in these territories
[Armenia] ; and in order to enable England to
make necessary provision for executing her
engagement [the keeping of Russia out of
Armenia], His Imperial Majesty, the Sultan,

further consents to assign the Island of Cyprus to be occupied and administered by England.'*

In July, 1878, on the motion of Lord Salisbury, the Congress adopted, in lieu of Article XVI. of the Treaty of San Stefano, the famous sixty-first Article of the Berlin Treaty. As thus remodelled, Russia was compelled to evacuate Armenia, and the Russian was exchanged for a European protectorate. A clause was introduced by which it

* 'The Anglo-Turkish Convention was in itself a gross and manifest breach of the public law of Europe. Because by the Treaty of Paris, the result of the Crimean War, it was solemnly enacted that everything that pertained to the integrity and independence of Turkey and to the relations between the Sultan and his subjects was matter not for the cognisance of one particular Power, but for the joint cognisance of the Great Powers of Europe. And what did we do in 1878? When the Russian War with Turkey came to a close we held Turkey rigidly to that principle. We insisted that the treaty she had made should be subject to the review of Europe, and that Europe should be entitled to a final judgment on these matters which fell within the scope of the Treaty of Paris. We did that, and we even wasted £6,000,000 in warlike preparations for giving effect to that declaration. We then brought together at Berlin, or assisted to bring together at Berlin, the Powers of Europe, for the purpose of exercising this supreme jurisdiction ; and while they were there, while they were at work, and without the knowledge of any one of them except Turkey, we extorted from the Sultan of Turkey—I am afraid by threatening him with abandoning the advocacy of his cause before the Congress—we extorted from the Sultan of Turkey the Anglo-Turkish Convention. But the Anglo-Turkish Convention was a convention which aimed at giving us power, in the teeth of the Treaty of Paris, between the Sultan and his subjects ; and it was a convention which virtually severed from his empire the possession of the island of Cyprus. It interfered with the integrity, it interfered with the independence. It broke the Treaty of Paris, and the Treaty of Paris was the public law of Europe.'—GLADSTONE, *Glasgow, December* 1, 1879.

was stipulated that Turkey will make known periodically the steps taken to carry out the reforms to the Powers, who will superintend their application.

The sixty-second Article of the treaty guarantees the largest possible measure of religious reform to all the Christian subjects of the Porte, including, of course, the Armenians.

A deputation of Armenians had attended the Congress, and expressed their views regarding the prospective reforms. They were at one in their joy over the advance that seemed to be made. Again the old men began to see visions and the young men to dream dreams.

The strategy and success of the plenipotentiaries of England at the Berlin Congress had been blazoned abroad before it was well known what had actually been done.

We hear now not a little of the apotheosis of Russia. In those halcyon times the apotheosis of Lord Beaconsfield and Lord Salisbury was the order of the day.*

The return of the diplomatists from Berlin was a red-letter day in the history of our country. A holiday crowd tumultuously cheered them on

---

* This was popularly expressed in one of the ballads of the day, thus :

> ' Ho, such a noise, for the Jingo boys
> Are shouting about like mad.
> Great Beaconsfield has made Europe yield
> To his every word and fad !'

their arrival at Dover. The ovation was continued along the route from Dover to Downing Street, and Lord Beaconsfield was saluted, in anticipation of new honours, as Duke of Cyprus.

The scene at Downing Street was dramatic in no ordinary degree. It was enlivened and rendered memorable by the closing performance of the two grand actors.

In response to a call from the jubilant crowd for a speech, Lord Beaconsfield stepped forward and said : ' Lord Salisbury and myself have brought you back Peace, but a Peace, I hope, with Honour, which may satisfy our Sovereign, and tend to the welfare of the country.' Lord Salisbury, who ' had pulled the labouring oar ' at the Congress, spoke in a similar buoyant strain, and was confident the British nation ' would always support a Government which supports the honour of England.'

Among the other trophies of this great diplomatic victory, the Cyprus White Elephant was frequently exhibited to admiring multitudes, and much applauded. Its suicidal tendency towards eating off its own head had not then been so generally suspected as to damp the popular enthusiasm in the acquisition of this new prodigy.

We may now, ere we leave our subject, take a parting glance at the region we have traversed far too hurriedly to mark more than a few points of outstanding prominence. We have seen the Powers of Europe—in the dark hour of Young

Armenia's distress at the failure of internal reform
on the basis of the Constitution of the Sultan—
come forward to her aid.   Their first service is
to steady the decrepit tyrant on his tottering
throne, and to put new strength into his palsied
hand, as well as a rod of iron by which he might
dash in pieces his enemies.   They then extort
from him promises of reform, all the time protesting they do not mean to interfere with his
internal affairs.   He, on the other hand, is ready
to throw himself into their arms, and of his own
spontaneous motion to convert his dominions
into an ideal Mohammedan paradise.   The winter
of discontent is now about to end for Armenia.
Her previous sufferings seem at last to have
purchased a long immunity from sorrow.   But
the delusion has begun to dispel.   The Sultan
was only in sport, playing a familiar and favourite
game with the infidel.

But the hour has come for a new departure.
The voice of war has been heard threatening
from a quarter where the thunder was never wont
to be mere stage thunder.   The Sultan is once
more upon his knees to the higher power.   He
is profuse in vows and prayers.   Yet all would
have been of little avail had not Europe come forward in what she deemed her own best interests
—to save him, or at least give him a respite, from
the impending doom.   Foremost among those
powers as accepting responsibility—and depriving
Armenia of the proffered services of Russia—

ranks our own British Empire. Henceforth more stringent conditions are imposed on the reforming Turk, and more ample guarantees are accepted for their fulfilment. We need not wonder that many were confident that a new era had at last dawned, and that the tragedy of Turkish misrule was drawing near its close.

The net outcome of that historical gathering at Berlin—as we were told by one of the most prominent members of the Congress, a master of epigrammatic phrase—was ' Peace with Honour.' Never assuredly was a political forecast more ignominiously discredited by. the sober truth of history.

CHAPTER VII.

Position of Armenia after the Treaty of Berlin—Bright
prospects — Turkish reforms — Attitude of European
Concert—Consular reports—Comments of British Press
— Hamidieh Cavalry—Sassoun massacres, 1894—New
reforms.

A T the close of the sittings of the Berlin
Congress Turkey was subjected to a
European Protectorate, which undertook
the grave responsibility of outlining and super-
vising certain reforms in the Ottoman Empire,
and above all in Armenia.

The Armenians were not mentioned in the
protocol of Adrianople, nor even in the Treaty of
San Stefano, until the omission, in the latter, was
supplied at the eleventh hour by the heroic inter-
position of their Patriarch Nerses. They were
included by name in the Treaty of Berlin, in the
61st Article, drawn up by Lord Salisbury, and
emphasis was laid upon their case in the terms of
the Cyprus Convention. And now, not only
youthful patriots, speaking through their mouth-
piece Nerses, but also aged and venerable
European statesmen began to indulge the vision
of a regenerated Armenia. The scattered families
of Haik were to reassemble around their long-

desolated firesides, and to restore the ruined
sanctuaries of the God of their fathers. Industry
and Commerce were again to lift up their heads.
Expeditions were to be furnished forth more
wondrous than that of Jason in search of the
golden fleece, and England was to act the part of
Medea.

It was hardly to be expected that Russia would
be so enthusiastic about the new order of things.
Her attitude might be expressed in the words
recently used by Prince Lobanoff to Sir F.
Lascelles that 'her direct interests on the frontier
forbade her to indulge in the philanthropic dreams
which seemed to prevail in England, whose
interests, on account of her insular position and
distance from the Armenian districts, were not
directly affected.'

Meantime, two things had become quite clear.
New and weighty obligations had been undertaken by the European Powers in the engagements of the Treaty of Berlin, and by England
in particular through her sacrifice of blood and
treasure along with France in the Crimean War
and the Cyprus Convention. These engagements,
to begin with, were avowed and gloried in as
triumphs of diplomacy by their chief author,
Lord Salisbury. But for long it has become the
fashion to ignore or disown them. On June 28,
1889, Lord Salisbury, in the House of Lords,
repudiated special responsibility. 'England,' he
said, 'is not the protector of Turkey, and cannot

exercise the rights of guardianship over her.'
Quite recently, in his speech at the Hotel
Metropole, he declared, referring to the 61st
Article of the Treaty of Berlin, and ignoring the
Cyprus Convention, that in it 'the six Powers
agree *not to any outside person*, but to each other,
that *if* the Sultan promulgates certain reforms,
they will watch over the execution of them.'   For
the improbable contingency of the conversion
of the Sultan, and of his government along
with him, Lord Salisbury, it thus appears,
sets aside the proffered services of the only
Christian power prepared to take forcible and
immediate measures to ensure these reforms.

The reforms were : protection of life and property, deliverance from an iniquitous system of
over taxation and civil disabilities, from personal
dishonour and from the evils of a despotism
modelled on the worst types of Moslem tyranny.
Did either Lord Salisbury, or any of the other
signatories of the Treaty, expect these reforms
from the Turk, whose independent action they so
jealously guarded from outside interference?   If
so, then—as we have already said—never was
political forecast more completely discredited by
the experience of the past, which they knew so
well, and in due time by the history of the future.
The disavowal of responsibility by Lord Salisbury for the carrying out of these reforms, must
be considered in the light of the actual provisions
of Treaty engagements, the *raison d'être* of our

occupation of Cyprus, and in the light of the record of British diplomacy at Constantinople, particularly as revealed in the authoritative statements of the Blue Books as far as these are available. We will glance at this record cursorily, keeping in view in particular the inquiries and results of Mr. M. G. Rolin-Jæquemyns, in his 'Armenia, the Armenians and the Treaties,' so far as the authoritative sources are available, *i.e.*, from 1879 to 1881, and then over a long period of official silence reluctantly broken by some comparatively brief utterances in 1889-90. We shall from this point refer mainly to the statements recently presented to both Houses of Parliament in the Blue Books relating to Turkey, 1896. These volumes contain correspondence respecting the Introduction of Reforms in the Armenian Provinces of Asiatic Turkey, correspondence relative to the Armenian Question and Reports from her Majesty's Consular Officers in Asiatic Turkey, and correspondence relating to the Asiatic Provinces of Turkey.

No satisfactory explanation has been given of the withholding of consular reports between 1881-89. Mr. Gladstone, in a speech in the House of Commons, May 28, 1889, speaks of it as the adoption, or liable to be confounded with, 'the adoption of the principle of eternal silence about the horrors that prevail in Armenia.'

Our cursory review will embrace three periods : (1) 1878-81, (2) 1881-89, (3) 1889—onwards.

As to the first period (1878-81).   This is a brief
season of initial efforts at reformation.   The consular reports were furnished from Eastern Turkey
by such highly competent authorities as Captains
Trotter and Everett (Erzeroum), Clayton (Mush),
Messrs. Wilson (Anatolia) and Chermside (Sivas),
etc.

Let us endeavour to get a bird's-eye view of
Armenia during these three years, when it was
just entering the political paradise whose prospective delights were inflaming the imagination of our
Western statesmen.

The Russo-Turkish war practically ceased with
the armistice, January 31, 1878.   Towards the
close of that year (December 21) Captain Trotter
reports that the present condition of Christians
throughout the district (except Diarbekir) is
' worse than it has been at any period during the
past several years.'*

In the provinces the rulers are of three grades :
the highest the vali (governor-general of vilayet
province), next the mutessarif (prefect of sandjak
districts), and, lowest, the kaimakam and mudir
(sub-prefects and mayors of casas, sub-districts, and
native parishes).   These rulers are often changed,
and get their appointments by bribery, and hence
they are tempted to recoup themselves from the
people as best they may, and so they, along with
the ill-paid or unpaid soldier and zaptieh, are the
official robbers of the provinces.

* Blue Book, Turkey, No. 10 (1879), p. 8.

On complaints of their depredations and outrages being made by the consuls to Lord Salisbury, and instructions requested as to how far the
consul was warranted to press reforms, Lord
Salisbury replies, May 21, 1879, referring to treaty
obligations: 'The Sultan is bound not only to
promulgate new and better laws, but to *actually
introduce* reforms.'* The Porte is again and again
warned by the British ambassador that if he do
not initiate reforms, he will create another Bulgaria in Asiatic Turkey, and this the moderate
Armenians do not desire. They only demand
protection to life and honour, and equal rights
with the Mussulmans. The grand vizier pleads in
excuse for inaction in reform the want of money.

In Western Turkey (Armenia Minor), and even
within a short distance of Constantinople, things
were as bad, or even worse, than farther east.
Here the plague of the Circassian refugees was
acting as a visitation of locusts, and one encouraged by the Sultan. The new region, the
creation of the genius mainly of English statesmen,
was turning out to be, not the Paradiso of their
dreams, but a veritable Inferno. The truth is, there
was another dreamer of dreams in the Yildiz kiosk.
Sultan Abdul Hamid, himself on the mother's side
an Armenian, and combining the worst qualities
of the Armenian and Moslem, was a true Oriental
visionary. When Turkey could no longer hold
out against Russia, there was a salve for the

* Blue Book, Turkey, No. 10 (1879), p. 76.

wounded national pride in a dream of the pious
Sultan. He saw the Prophet in a vision of the
night, and was told by him that enough Russians
had been killed. Abdul Hamid also saw a vision
of himself as an ideal Moslem despot and patron
saint of Islam. The character and ideals of
Abdul Hamid enter as an important factor into
the working-out of the entire problem known as
the Eastern Question.

What, then, is the normal aspect of the Turkish
régime, as we may trace it in its influence on the
national life of Turkey so ruled, and as it still
continues to exist? This bears on finance, justice,
police, and central and local government. Mr.
Rolin-Jæquemyns conclusively proves that all
these departments are radically corrupt. There
is no end to oppressive taxation, abuses of the
law of the hospitality tax, and no account of mal-
treatment of non-Moslems will ever be taken as
long as the valis are able to honour the *havales*, or
money-orders, of the Sultan. The mal-administra-
tion of justice arises partly from the evils inherent
in the legal system, especially of the Sheriat
Courts, but chiefly from the low character of its
administrators. 'The first consideration of the
administrator of justice,' says Mr. Everett, 'is
the amount of money that can be extorted from
an individual, and the second is his creed; for it
is an established principle, which in fact guides
the conduct of a court throughout a trial, that a
favourable decision shall be given to him who will

pay the most for it, some abatement being allowed
under certain circumstances to a Mohammedan
when engaged in a suit with a Christian.'* As
to the condition of the police and gendarmerie, no
improvements were made. ' The old system with
all its abuses obtains 't (Chermside). Mr. Everett
thus describes this old system : ' Firstly, there are
not sufficient police ; secondly, there are no good
officers; and, thirdly, there is collusion between
the local authorities and the robbers.'‡ We will
not comment on the evils of either central or
local administration farther than to say that the
whole system is an organized hypocrisy, wearing
the garb and, so far as possible, using the
phraseology of the civilization of the nineteenth
century.

But had the European concert really done
nothing during this period to promote reform ?
Had England made no effort to redeem her
pledges ? In 1879 a British squadron was
ordered to the Archipelago to enforce the stipulated reforms. The Sultan took alarm and promised everything. In June, 1880, an identical
note (and again in September of the same year, a
collective note of the Powers) demanded the
execution of the stipulations, declaring that ' the
interest of Europe as well as of the Ottoman
Empire requires the observance of the sixty-first

* Blue Book, Turkey, No. 8 (1881), p. 109.
† *Ibid.*, No. 6 (1881), p. 91.
‡ *Ibid.*, p. 186.

Article of the Treaty of Berlin, and that the joint and incessant action of the Powers can alone bring about this result.' The Sultan replied to this appeal renewing his former pledges, and hinting that his government was the unfortunate subject of persistent prejudice and calumny. In 1881 Earl Granville made an effort to induce the Powers to unite in a further remonstrance, but without success. Both France and Germany saw ' serious inconvenience ' in raising the Armenian question. The effect of this attitude was to postpone indefinitely all collective action of the Powers on behalf of Armenia.

The period 1881-89 is one of diplomatic silence. The conversion of the Sultan has not proved so easy a matter as was supposed, and the pressure upon him of the signatories of the Treaty of Berlin is relaxed. Things are allowed to drift. Bismark, as we have seen, deemed it well to let the Armenian question rest for a time, and France acquiesced. Russia professed to be full of devotion to the cause of the liberties of the Armenians, but could not forget the Turkish Convention, and the foolish jubilations to which it gave rise in England.

The concert of Europe—crossed as it was by this isolated action on the part of England—instead of prosecuting reforms in Armenia, busied itself in carrying out the twenty-fourth Article of the Treaty regarding the rectification of the frontier between Greece and Montenegro.

The temper of Turkish rule in Asia Minor during this period, no doubt fostered by the inaction of the Powers, is illustrated by such examples as the assassination by a band of Kurds of two inoffensive American citizens, Messrs. Knapp and Reynolds (1883), while travelling through the eastern districts. The ambassador of the United States met with insulting treatment on his visit to the grand vizier anent this outrage. The Turkish government neither acknowledged communications from the American Government, nor took any notice of the indemnity demanded for the murderous assault.

During this season of their dumb sorrows the Armenians suffered more than before the treaty from the ravages of Turks, Kurds and Circassians, from repression of all liberty of thought and action, and the deprivation of the most elementary rights of citizenship. We shall not further seek at this stage to withdraw the veil which the tender mercies of our government cast over the horror-stricken countenances of the Armenians as they gradually awoke to the discovery of the betrayal of their hopes and aspirations.

But the diplomatic narrative is resumed in the third and last period of our brief review. A very cursory glance over the pages of the Blue Books of 1895-96 will enable us to trace the main current of events, and the general character of the correspondence between this country and the chief parties concerned in the interests of Armenia.

The Armenians, it is evident, were systematically oppressed and degraded.   Their patient endurance of wrong is one of their most striking characteristics.   What the Turk stigmatized as rebellion was nothing else than a protest against intolerable tyranny.   The simple expression of dissatisfaction in any form with the imperial modes of oppression was insurrection.   ' I believe,' says Mr. Clifford Lloyd, consul at Erzeroum (October 2, 1890), ' that the idea of revolution is not entertained by any class of the Armenian people in these provinces, whatever may be the aims of those outside them.   An armed revolution is, besides, impossible.'   The official reports from consul and ambassador bear ample witness to the fictitious crimes charged upon the Armenians, and the appalling numbers of wanton arrests on groundless suspicion, or pretext of suspicion. Sometimes, under a burning sense of ' the inexpiable wrong, the unutterable shame,' or other fiendish outrage for which there was no redress, an avenger appeared who did exact the penalty of the crime without the formalities of Ottoman law, and this was, of course, entirely unconstitutional.

In reference to the arrest of a large number of Armenian suspects—over three-score—about the Narman district for the murder of four Turkish brigands, Consul Hampson says : ' It appears to me indisputable that the origin of all this trouble is the neglect of the local government to secure

the proper punishment of the murderers of the
three Armenians last year.'*

Only less obnoxious to the Sultan than these
Armenian rebellions were the frank utterances of
the English Press. To that Briarean monster
the same drastic treatment could not, of course,
be applied, as would have been the case had his
headquarters been in Constantinople. The *Daily
News*, it seems, had been grossly exaggerating the
number of political prisoners in Erzeroum, Van,
and Mush. The veracious Turkish officials could
only be brought to own over one half of the
number of the 700 alleged political suspects or
others charged with political crimes, in prison.†
Side by side with Abdul Hamid's denunciations
of the British Press came the decoration of
Zekki Pasha, his chief agent in the Sassoun
massacres, and the silk banners with which he
rewarded the zeal of the Kurdish chiefs.

Just as the Valis of Eastern Asiatic Turkey are
reporting, after a tour of inspection of their
provinces, that all is tranquil, the military reserves

* Blue Book, No. 3 (1896), p. 3.
† Blue Book, No. 2 (1896), p. 57. The following extract
from a report by the Hon. R. Lister on the prisons of Constantinople (October 17, 1895), clearly proves how utterly
worthless are the statements of Turkish officials on such
matters. 'His excellency (the Turkish minister of police),
stated that only 170 Armenians had been arrested, but this
is palpably untrue, as I myself saw 299.' Mr. Lister's report
relates to an official inspection of the prisons of Constantinople immediately after the disturbances there, and he is
specially thanked for it by Lord Salisbury.

are being mysteriously mobilized. There are con-
jectures as to the meaning of this. In Western
Turkey (Armenia Minor), the Bishop of Zeitoun
and his fellow suspects, after an imprisonment
of sixteen months, are undergoing their mock
trial.

The reforming Turk is manifestly not idle.
Meantime, Lord Salisbury writes as follows to the
new ambassador at Constantinople—Sir Clare
Ford—March 17, 1892 : 'I think it desirable, on
the occasion of your assumption of the duties of
Her Majesty's Ambassador to the Sultan, to invite
your excellency's attention to the question of the
condition of the Asiatic provinces of Turkey, and
to the correspondence on the subject which is in
the Embassy archives. Owing to the difficulty of
securing any concerted action in the matter by
the Powers parties to the Treaty of Berlin, Her
Majesty's Government *have of late years desisted
from urging upon the Porte the introduction of
general reforms in fulfilment of its obligations under
Article LXI. of that Treaty*, and have confined
themselves to bringing to the notice of the Sultan's
ministers the most prominent instances of misgovernment and outrage which have been reported
by her Majesty's consular officers. Her Majesty's
Government would wish your Excellency to continue to act on these lines.'*

The scheme of the creation of the military
Militia—now notorious as the Hamidieh Cavalry

* Blue Book, No. 3 (1896), p. 8. *Ibid.*, pp. 24, 34.

—had been launched in the previous year. 'The initiative of this happy idea,' says the official announcement, 'and the great success which will certainly crown its execution, are due to the wisdom and foresight of his Imperial Majesty the Sultan.'

The Kurdish chiefs indulged in some preliminary massacres among their own tribes, arising from disputes about precedency, and by way of preparation for their grand mission. That mission was to see that no evil consequences resulted from the Turkish reforms, and, in brief, to substitute as quickly as possible a Kurdish for an Armenian population on the borders of Russia and Persia.

These, in the case of a Cossack invasion, would be likely to form a more reliable barrier than the evil-affected infidel. By the middle of 1892, Zekki Pasha (the Marshal of the 4th Army Corps) is busy organizing, enrolling and presenting colours to the Hamidieh regiments. The consul at Diarbekir states that the Marshal had a brilliant reception, and that 'the Hamidieh regiments in their new uniform looked very smart and soldier-like, and their behaviour during their stay here was every way orderly.'

Zekki Pasha is able to announce at Van (in June) that full forty regiments of Kurds had been formed, which would give a body of some 20,000 cavalry. A detailed description of this brigand militia is given by Colonel Chermside in his report to the British Ambassador, December 15, 1892.

In vain did the Armenians of Mush and other districts, discerning too well the meaning of these movements, appeal for timely protection. The policy of non-interference, in which Lord Salisbury had been indoctrinating the representatives of our government, was absolutely fatal to all such appeals. As a matter of fact, the outcry of alarm was unheeded.

The Turk did indeed confess that things were unsettled, but he was doing his best to remedy all grievances. When his attention was drawn to the ill-treatment, by his creatures, of the English traveller, Rev. C. H. Robinson—who could not help being an eye-witness of Moslem outrages, and whose testimony there was good reason to dread—his Majesty could not believe his ears, that his people would show any other feeling than true Moslem respect to 'that great and friendly nation.'

The year 1893 is a period of revolutionary scares in the Turkish Empire. For such a time the Hamidieh were called into existence, and it must come. Early in the year seditious placards were displayed in Marsovan, Amassia, Tokat, Angora, Diarbekir, and elsewhere.

The Turkish Government suspected the Armenians as the authors. Then followed a tragedy of oppression of an innocent people, to discover among them the evidence of disaffection to the government. The houses of the people were ransacked, their inmates outraged, and wholesale arrests were made on suspicion. Marsovan and the neighbouring districts were regarded as the chief centres of the insurrection. The Turkish leader set fire, it was supposed, to the American college at Marsovan, and then charged the missionaries as being the incendiaries.

The placards—the main cause of these atrocities—emanated, it was believed, by those best qualified to form a judgment, not from the Armenians, but from the Moslems themselves.

The Armenians were, no doubt, in course of time implicated, and perhaps used as tools in the movement. They were instigated and misled, so far as they could be induced to adopt questionable methods, by foreign influence from Armenian committees in Athens, Geneva, Marseilles, Paris, and London.

The truth was, there were two revolutions of somewhat different complexions in progress in Turkey—the one Moslem, the other Armenian. The leaders of the former, *i.e.*, the Softas (theological students) recently expelled from Constantinople, and now scattered through the provinces, were probably the authors of the seditious placards which led to the arrest of some 1,800 Armenian suspects, and to what Lord Rosebery designates as the cruel farce of the Angora trials.

'It is more than probable,' writes Consul Longworth, 'that with some kind of Armenian

association a Moslem secret society exists, or
perhaps co-operates.'*

The Armenian rebellion, we doubt not, when
the drama has been played out, will yet be regarded as a noble movement of the ancient
national spirit—not always, indeed, wisely guided
as to its methods—towards that freedom for which
our own Empire had at one time to struggle
through prisons and inquisitions and star-cham-
bers, amid the gruesome orgies of the scaffold
and the stake. But these are rather high-flown
sentiments, for, after all, what right have these
dogs of Nazarenes to move their tongues against
the immaculate Moslem? Why should they not
suffer in silence—die, and make no sign? Alas!
the tragedy of the year 1894 makes it only too
plain that this is what thousands of this unhappy
people have done, and are still doing!

In 1894 took place the massacres of Sassoun,
when, under the command of Zekki Pasha, the
Turkish soldiers, along with their Hamidieh con-

* Blue Book, No. 3 (1896), p. 121. The following para-
graph appeared recently in the newspapers: The Press
Association says : 'An appeal to European nations has
been issued by the Turkish Reform League, in which a
plan of campaign is outlined for the deposition of the Sultan.
Having appealed to Germany and England in turn, the
reformers implore Europe for aid, even if it should result in
breaking up the Ottoman Empire. The only means, they
declare, of releasing the Empire from its horrible misrule is
the speedy removal of the tyrant Caliph. European Governments, had they the will, could force the Dardanelles, and,
surrounding Yildiz Kiosk with marines, depose the Sultan,
placing him on board a gunboat, and not twenty lives would
be lost in the resistance of the Palace Guard.'

tingent, entered with due formality upon the work of avowed extermination of the Armenians. The abbot of Mush informed the British consul at Erzeroum of the forthcoming onslaught, but, as we have already said, the British Government could not interfere with the internal affairs of a friendly nation.

Mr. Greene gives a graphic picture of these blood-curdling scenes in his chapter of horrors on the evidence of reliable witnesses. 'The Turks,' says Dr. Dillon, 'in their confidential moods, have admitted these and worse acts of savagery ; the Kurds glory in them at all times ; trustworthy Europeans have witnessed and described them, and Armenians groaned over them in blank despair. Officers and nobles in the Sultan's own cavalry regiments, like Mostigo the Kurd, bruit abroad with unpardonable pride the story of the long series of rapes and murders which marked their official careers, and laugh to scorn the notion of being punished for robbing and killing the Armenians, whom the Sublime Porte desires them to exterminate.'*

The bare outline of the narrative is somewhat as follows. In May, 1893, a revolutionist named Damatian was captured in the neighbourhood of Mush, and thrown into the now notorious Bitlis prison. The whole district of Mush and Talvoreeg was declared to be in a state of scarcely veiled rebellion. No doubt there was inability to pay

* *Contemporary Review*, January, 1896. 'Armenia : an Appeal.'

double taxes—first to Kurds, and then to the government. Even if there were few or any agitators in this district, there was an undue preponderance of Armenians, and therefore a necessity for diminishing the population. It is, it seems, a suggestive fact that the Turks, as a race, are becoming extinct, while the Armenians under normal circumstances are a growing people. The Turkish debauchee cannot keep pace as to increase of his kind with his Armenian vassal, and hence the periodic massacre, at least if stronger measures cannot be adopted.

More plausible pretexts, however, had to be sought for so gigantic an undertaking as the extermination of the Armenian population of Sassoun. It was of course forthcoming; the Turk is never long at a loss in such a case. Some Kurdish brigands, coming ostensibly to collect double taxes, carried off as an incident of the visit—and a quite commonplace incident—a few of the cattle of the impoverished villagers. The Armenians, in the struggle to recover their property and means of livelihood, killed four Kurdish brigands. This, beyond doubt, was rebellion, and orders were forthwith issued from Constantinople to the soldiery, Kurds included, to destroy utterly every Armenian—man, woman and child—in the rebel district. It is said that Zekki Pasha read to his motley host these orders, and hung the royal firman as an ornament upon his breast.

In August, 1894, began that awful ordeal of

indiscriminate massacre of man, woman and child in the Sassoun district, estimated (though the exact number can now never be known) at 15,000, some placing the figures lower and others much higher.

We shall give only a single picture of this Mohammedan saturnalia, drawn for us by one of the correspondents of Mr. Greene whose veracity is beyond suspicion. 'The region was surrounded by soldiers of the army, and 20,000 Kurds also are said to have been massed there. Then they advanced upon the centre, driving in the people like a flock of sheep, and continued thus to advance for days. No quarter was given, no mercy shown—men, women and children shot down or butchered like sheep. Probably, when they were set upon in this way, some tried to save their lives and resisted in self-defence. Many who could fled in all directions, but the majority were slain. The most probable estimate is 15,000 killed, thirty-five villages plundered, razed, burnt. Women were outraged and then butchered; a priest taken to the roof of his church and hacked to pieces; young men piled in with wood saturated with kerosene and set on fire; a large number of women and girls collected in church, kept for days, violated by the brutal soldiers, and then murdered.'

Such were the Sassoun massacres, and yet it has been pathetically declared by those who have good reason to know best that the butchery of Sassoun is but a drop in the ocean of Armenian blood shed gradually and silently over the empire since the late Turko-Russian war.

As a sulky concession to the advice of the Powers, a commission was appointed by the Sultan to proceed to the scene of the disturbances and inquire. Those who knew anything of the reforming Turk were able to appraise this concession at its proper value. The commission was a diplomatic expedient, in default of a better, to entertain the facile concert of Europe with a little grim comedy in the interludes of a too horrible tragedy, planned and now being executed before their eyes on a scale of unprecedented magnitude.

While the civilized world was still under the shock of the revelations of Sassoun, neither the Sultan nor his ministers seemed aware that anything unusual had taken place. On March 28, 1895, the Earl of Kimberley, in reference to an interview with Rustem Pasha at the Foreign Office, writes to Sir P. Currie : ' His Excellency spoke with much bitterness of what he considered were the exaggerated and unfounded statements of the atrocities alleged to have been committed by the Turkish soldiers in the Sassoun district.'* A discreet silence as to the atrocities became the order of the day all round, broken at times by a euphemistic allusion to the ' Sassoun occurrences ' by the Sultan, or by an incredulous inquiry on the part of the grand vizier whether our ambassador

* Blue Book, No. 1 (1896), p. 12.

really thought there ever had been any Sassoun massacres.* Hints were indeed thrown out by our representatives that the neglect of the Turkish Government to exact punishment from the criminals of Sassoun notoriety was making a bad impression in England and in Europe.

This state of things the Turk could not understand, but, as it could not be entirely ignored, he would make inquiry. The year 1895 is largely a year of discussion of projected reforms in Turkey. One of the Blue Books submitted this year is devoted, we may say, wholly to the subject of these reforms, to which it gives 176 folio pages. They are somewhat wearisome reading, and we can only indicate their general current. The scheme of reforms originates with our British Ambassador, no doubt inspired from Downing Street. It is considered by the other ambassadors, and generally approved. The Powers give, in due course, their approval after modification, and with varying degrees of cordiality. Prince Lobanoff would concur, but he does not think there is now an Armenia. He has made inquiries and received conflicting accounts. He at last gives way, on condition that England does not intend to create a new Armenia or Bulgaria in Asiatic Turkey.

In the meantime the Sultan has appointed another Commission to draw up a counter-scheme of still better reforms. When the scheme of the ambassadors is laid before him he cautiously sets

* Blue Book, No. 1 (1896), p. 16.

it aside, first for consideration, then for rejection.
Encouraged by the attitude of Prince Lobanoff,
who objects decisively to pressure on the Sultan,
compelling him to adopt the reforms, he gets
bolder, and makes an effort to sow dissension
among the European Powers. The German
Emperor is approached to use his influence to
moderate the pressure of the other Powers, but
in vain.

In the meantime, Lord Salisbury, on his accession to power, is careful to inform Rustem Pasha
that he supports entirely the policy which his
government had inherited from their predecessors
in office.*

His Lordship then shows considerable anxiety
to convince Prince Lobanoff that England will not
coerce the Sultan, and will not give autonomy in
any form to the Armenians. The Russian minister,
who, manifestly, is not prodigal of compliments,
takes occasion at this unwonted and somewhat
pathetic spectacle of the climbing down of the
English Premier, to express his admiration of the
moderate and statesmanlike attitude he had now
assumed. The lion and the bear were at last
about to lie down together. Disputes about commissions of control and commissions of surveil-
lance were at an end. Under these fostering
auspices Turkey gets a somewhat freer hand to
reduce the reforms into their final shape. In
October, 1895, the imperial iradé is issued, sanc-

* Blue Book, No. 1 (1896), p. 94.

tioning the new scheme of reforms, granting new political privileges to the Armenians of the vilayets of Erzeroum, Sivas Van, Diarbekir, Bitlis, and Mamouret-el-Aziz. The reforms are set forth with a flourish of Moslem trumpets as the embodiment of the glorious provisions of the Hatti-Humayoun, and as proceeding spontaneously from his imperial Majesty the Sultan.

The Valis are duly instructed to carry out the matters decided upon with extraordinary zeal, attention, and care in their districts, and to report in due course upon the results thus obtained.

From all these airy phantoms the imagination cannot help reverting to the actual state of things. We emerge from the region of fancy to find the blissful dream of Young Armenia replaced by a waking vision of saddest reality. As we glance back over the period we have been so cursorily reviewing, we see the good resolutions and solemn pledges of the Sultan succeeded by the most diabolical measures in defiance of civilization, and the most shameless breach of faith which has ever disgraced the history of any political power.

We have noted the descent to the nadir of Moslem oppression—in the elaborate preparations and first gigantic butchery, in the projected extermination of the Turkish Armenian.

We have surveyed from afar the region of the shadow of death. The one redeeming aspect of this doleful spectacle is the martyr spirit, the martyr courage, of the brave Armenian sufferers. When the simple acceptance of the creed of Islam would have saved them from all their present woes, they elected to abide by the faith of Christ, and to seal their testimony with their blood.

CHAPTER VIII.

Renewal of massacres, 1895-96—The Hindchag's Communication to the Embassies—Collective Note—Illustrative cases—Trebizond and Ourfa—Attitude of Prince Lobanoff—Responsibility for the massacres—Relation of the European Powers—The special responsibility of Great Britain—Question not closed—Solutions of the problem —Conclusion.

WHEN, after announcing his purpose of introducing his grand scheme of reforms, the Sultan expressed amazement that Lord Salisbury did not telegraph grateful thanks—he is reminded that his lordship had been on the outlook for the publication of the measures of reform, and was disappointed at the unaccountable delay. As the exchange of diplomatic courtesies proceeds the Sultan becomes hopeful that England must at last be satisfied with what he has done, but is reminded that much will depend on how the paper reforms are actually carried out.

Nothing, indeed, is more melancholy than the history of one of the Sultan's reformations, even as it may be traced in the unimpassioned consular reports. The reformation is the euphuism for a fresh outbreak of fanaticism on the part of the

Turk, and means, so far as the Armenians are concerned, another serious attempt at their extermination.

When Mr. Hampson, Vice-Consul at Mush, visits, in the month of August, five or six villages in that district, to make inquiries as to the truth of reports about the misconduct of the tax-collectors, a complaint has to be made to the Grand Vizier that the Turkish authorities had put every possible hindrance in his way so that he might not get at the facts. This unfriendly treatment is sufficiently explained by the results of such investigations as Mr. Hampson was able to make. In every village where he went he witnessed the most appalling scenes of misery inflicted by the Turks and Kurds, and was surrounded by crowds of men, women, and children whose cry was ever the same—' Save us from the brutalities of the zaptiehs, save us from Reshid Effendi.' Reshid Effendi was the miscreant who was Captain of the Police. The outrages of the zaptiehs, under his orders, are thus referred to by the Vice-Consul in his report: ' Men are beaten, imprisoned, . . . women and girls are insulted and dishonoured, dragged naked from their beds at night; children are not spared, and these outrages are merely the amusement of the zaptiehs while engaged in selling the little remaining property of the villages at a quarter of its value.' Such are the pleasantries which lighten the toil of the official tax-gatherer among the impoverished, starving Armenians. At each fresh outrage the zaptiehs jeeringly tell the sufferers, ' Now go and complain to your foreign consuls !'*

While these sickening scenes were being prolonged the ' Hindchag,' the Armenian Revolutionary Committee, addressed a communication to the Ambassadors at Constantinople, stating that a strictly peaceful demonstration was to be held, to express their desire for the carrying out of the promised reforms. A petition was drawn up protesting against admitted and clamant wrongs and demanding the long-deferred redress. In that touching appeal they refer to the Sassoun massacres, and declare that they have waited patiently for a whole year for some ' prompt and effective solution from the Powers which signed the Treaty of Berlin.'

The demonstration came off in Constantinople in the end of September and beginning of October. It was, of course, magnified into a daring rebellion, and such were the cruelties perpetrated upon the Armenians, whether implicated in the riot or otherwise, that the Powers took the unusual step of a remonstrance with the Sultan in the form of a collective Note.

This Note is as mild in tone and substance as diplomacy could make it. The outrages are referred to as 'regrettable incidents.' It is, however, distinctly declared that the excesses of the

* Blue Book, Turkey, No. 2 (1896), p. 17.

Turk cannot be excused, and 'will not fail to arouse the indignation of Europe if it becomes apparent that the supineness of the authorities is encouraging regrettable passions.'

But the massacres were once more the order of the day. The immunity with which the government had conducted their bold experiment of the Sassoun massacres had given them fresh courage to prosecute their policy. Threats were heard—and they were no empty words—of coming horrors, beside which the slaughter of Sassoun would sink into insignificance.

In the month of October broke out the massacres at Trebizond. For these it was found on investigation there was no cause arising from the insurrectionary action of the Armenians. Some 600 were tortured and vivisected at the outset. The plunder amounted to at least £200,000. The disturbances spread to Erzeroum and other parts of Eastern Turkey. But they did not stop there. The Turks and Circassians were already turning the Armenian centres in the West into a hell upon earth. Passions and appetites to which the very fiends of the pit are strangers, were freely indulged in the light of day and amid the sanctities of the domestic circle. The tragedies of Zeitoun, Marash, Ourfa, Aintab, and others, are no doubt fresh in the recollection of the reader.

Into the details of these we cannot go. A tabular statement at the close of Blue Book, Turkey, No. 2, gives an official estimate of the numbers of the slaughtered victims during this period.

The character of the crimes invented and perpetrated on the hapless Armenians baffles all description. Yet an incident which can be related here and there reveals the nature of the ordeal of unutterable woe. We shall only venture upon two cases, by way of illustration, not worse than hundreds and thousands of similar tragedies. They occurred the one at Trebizond, and the other at Ourfa.

'In Trebizond,' says Dr. E. J. Dillon, 'on the first day of the massacre, an Armenian was coming out of a baker's shop, where he had been purchasing bread for his sick wife and family, when he was surprised by the raging crowd. Fascinated with terror, he stood still, was seized, and dashed to the ground. He pleaded piteously for mercy and pardon, and they quietly promised it ; and so grim and dry was the humour of this crowd that the trembling wretch took their promise seriously, and offered them his heartfelt thanks. In truth, they were only joking. When they were ready to be serious, they tied the man's feet together, and taunted him, but at first with the assumed gentleness that might well be mistaken for the harbinger of mercy. Then they cut off one of his hands, slapped his face with the bloody wrist, and placed it between his quivering lips. Soon afterwards they chopped off the other hand, and inquired whether he would like pen and

paper to write to his wife. Others requested him
to make the sign of the Cross with his stumps, or
with his feet, while he still possessed them, while
others desired him to shout louder that his God
might hear his cries for help. One of the most
active members of the crowd then stepped forward
and tore the man's ears from his head, after which
he put them between his lips, and then flung them
in his face. "That Effendi's mouth deserves to be
punished for refusing such a choice morsel," exclaimed a voice in the crowd, whereupon some-
body stepped forward, knocked out some of his
teeth, and proceeded to cut out his tongue. "He
will never blaspheme again," a pious Moslem
jocosely remarked. Thereupon a dagger was
placed under one of his eyes, which was scooped
clean out of its socket. The hideous contortions
of the man's discoloured face, the quick convul-
sions of his quivering body, and the sight of the
ebbing blood turning the dry dust to gory mud,
literally intoxicated these furious fanatics, who,
having gouged out his other eye and chopped off
his feet, hit upon some other excruciating tortures
before cutting his throat and sending his soul " to
damnation," as they expressed it. These other
ingenious, pain-sharpening devices, however, were
such as do not lend themselves to description.'*

The brutal fanaticism of the Ourfa massacre
may be gathered from the following extract from

* *Contemporary Review*, January, 1896. 'Armenia : an
Appeal' (Dillon).

the Report of Vice-Consul Fitzmaurice to Sir P. Currie, dated Ourfa, March 16, 1896:

' A few shots were fired, and a trumpet sounded the attack from among the soldiers, who were seen to open their ranks and allow the mob behind them to come forward. Soldiers and mob then rushed on the Armenian quarter, and began a general massacre of the males over a certain age.

'The reserve troops, who knew the Armenian quarter well from their having been on guard there during the two preceding months, served both as guides and advance guard, being accompanied by a body of woodcutters, axe in hand, from the neighbouring mountains. The latter broke in the doors, whereupon the soldiers rushed in, emptying their Martinis on the Armenian men, from whom they had anticipated a certain resistance. They had, however, given up all their arms, and, in abject terror at their dreadful situation, pleaded for mercy for the sake of their women and children and the Prophet Jesus. With insulting language they were dragged out one by one from their hiding-places and brutally butchered. In many instances from fifteen to twenty men had collected in the larger houses, as affording some chance of safety. They were hurled out one after another to the executioners, who speedily dispatched them. In the house next to that of the Protestant pastor (he, too, was slain, leaving six orphans), where I put up during my stay here, forty men were thus put to death. A certain Sheikh ordered his

followers to bring as many stalwart young
Armenians as they could find. They were, to the
number of about 100, thrown on their backs, and
held down by their hands and feet, while the
Sheikh, with a combination of fanaticism and
cruelty, proceeded, while reciting verses of the
Koran, to cut their throats after the Mecca rite of
sacrificing sheep.

'The savage butchery of the previous day (*i.e.*,
Saturday) was continued till noon, when took
place the burning of the Ourfa Armenian Cathedral, an act which for fiendish barbarity has been
unsurpassed by any of the horrors of recent
massacres of Armenians, and for which the annals
of history can furnish few, if any, parallels.

'On Saturday night crowds of Armenian men,
women and children took refuge in their fine
Cathedral, capable of holding some 8,000 persons,
and the priest administered the sacrament—the
last sacrament as it proved to be—to 1,800 souls,
recording the figure on one of the pillars of the
church. These remained in the Cathedral over-
night, and were joined on Sunday by several
hundreds more, who sought the protection of a
building which they considered safe from the mob-
violence of the Mussulman even in his fanaticism.
It is computed that at least 3,000 individuals
were congregated in this edifice when the mob
attacked it.

'They at first fired in through the windows, then
smashed in the iron door, and proceeded to

massacre all those, mostly men, who were on the
ground-floor. . . . Having collected a quantity of
bedding and the church matting, they poured
some thirty cans of kerosene on it, as also on the
dead bodies lying about, and then set fire to the
whole. The gallery beams and wooden frame-
work soon caught fire, whereupon, blocking up
the staircases leading to the gallery with similar
inflammable materials, they left the mass of
struggling human beings to become the prey of
the flames.

'During several hours the sickening odour of
roasted flesh pervaded the town, and even to-day,
two months and a half after the massacre, the
smell of putrescent and charred remains in the
church is unbearable.'

Vice-Consul Fitzmaurice, as appears from his
despatch given in the latest papers submitted to
Parliament (and carrying down the official statement to the 26th May, 1896), expresses his belief
that the Central Government is the real author of
these massacres. He adds : ' The general position
of the Armenians here and in the surrounding
country, if not indeed in the Asiatic provinces of
the empire, is deplorable. They are practically
considered as outlaws.'

But we have been somewhat anticipating what
remains of our now closing survey.

In November last year (1895) Lord Salisbury
again presses upon the Sultan a little more good
advice about the reforms. He takes note of his

Majesty's friendship for this country, and does his
best to assure him that the feeling is reciprocated
in high quarters, as well as that Great Britain
means to assist him in well-doing. At the same
time there is not wanting something of that
candour which is the privilege of friendship, and
which, amid all these honeyed words, supplies the
sting of a little wholesome sincerity. 'The fact,'
says his lordship, 'that the Sultan recently
decorated an officer whom he had dismissed on
the ground of gross misgovernment does not
encourage her Majesty's Government to feel any
confidence in the earnestness of his Imperial
Majesty's intentions to give serious effect to the
promised measures of reform.'*

Prince Lobanoff is quite sure, from his experience in the East, that such disturbances as
are occurring in Turkey, when unsupported by
outside influence, soon die a natural death, and
throws upon England the blame of the Constantinople and other massacres. England has
been encouraging insurrection!

Under such auspices we need not wonder that
the Powers do not see their way to interfere with
the internal affairs of Turkey. This, says Prince
Lobanoff, would be a violation of Article IX. of
the Treaty of Paris, and Article LXIII. of the
Treaty of Berlin. Treaty of Paris, and all the
rest, Russia was more than ready in 1878, had
the Powers not interdicted, to have kept her

* Blue Book, Turkey, No. 2 (1896), p. 122.

Cossacks in Turkey, and coerced the Sultan as to internal reforms.

To Prince Lobanoff the Sultan now appears as a glorified incarnation of reform, only he must be let alone, or rather assisted in carrying out his benevolent designs. Russia, he is confident, would not sanction any course of action which wore the aspect of a European interference.

Anything more callous, more distinctly a betrayal of the oppressed Armenians, than the memorandum in which Prince Lobanoff refuses to co-operate with the Powers to secure deliverance for these and other victims of Moslem outrage, it would be hard to find even in the records of Turkish diplomacy.*

As to the general question of responsibility for the ever-recurring massacres, the Turk would, of course, lay the entire blame on the Armenians and their abettors. The Armenians are rebels. This charge, however, has, as we have seen, been refuted over and over again by the most definite statements as to their non-revolutionary, law-abiding character by such authorities as Consuls Clifford, Lloyd, Chermside, Hampson, etc. It is, indeed, admitted that the brutal treatment to which they are subjected is producing disaffection.

The responsibility for the misrule and massacres

* The recent expressions of the mind of Russia through Prince Lobanoff, and his general tone adopted towards our Government, make it somewhat difficult to accept the pleasing theory of the brilliant authoress of 'Russia and England' as to the traditional policy of Russia, in its bearing on the relations of the two countries.

of the Armenians is no doubt primarily to be charged on the Sultan and his creatures. · There is abundant evidence that the arming of the Kurds and Circassians are only new developments in the traditional policy of wholesale slaughter. It was clearly foreseen by the Armenians and others before the outbreak of the recent series of massacres. Vain attempts also were made to induce the Powers, and especially our own English Government, to lay an arrest on the movement. The lifting of a finger by the arbiters of his fate would have saved the frantically appealing victim ; but it was not done.

The European Powers, as all the world knows, have contracted a special responsibility, not only on grounds of common humanity, but of definite treaty engagements. The setting aside of the provisions of the Treaty of San Stefano, and the substitution of those of the Treaty of Berlin, was the replacing of a Turco-Russian by a Turco-European undertaking.

The Turk has, especially of late, had the effrontery, when pressed to remedy gross abuses, to inquire what right England has to interfere with her internal affairs. When the Turkish Ambassador proposed this innocent query to Lord Kimberley, his lordship referred him for answer to the 61st Article of the Treaty of Berlin. Whatever may be Lord Salisbury's present reading of that Article, there certainly was a time when he would have taken no lower ground.

But it is not only England that has come under special obligations : all the European Powers—signatories of the Treaty of Berlin—have undertaken the most solemn engagements in regard to Turkish reforms. They are each and all partners in a common trust, which, to the disgrace of the civilization of Christian Europe, they have, through their mutual jealousies, or from whatever cause, most ignominiously betrayed. Such is the grave, yet absolutely truthful, indictment. Of no one Power may this be separately true, as the responsibility is collective rather than individual, but it is certainly true of the European Concert as a whole.

The apportioning of blame where each has a share is a delicate task. It would seem as if Russia had so far departed from her traditional *rôle* of protector of her oppressed co-religionist in Turkey as to have decided to leave him to the tender mercies of a tyrant whose astutely-planned policy, she knows, is to outrage, torture, and crush him out of existence.

We may do less than justice to the other European Powers, but we hardly think we can have any treacherous bias against our own English Government. We assuredly do not object to any place of prominence the English nation may assume in regard to the solution of the gravest problem of the civilization of the nineteenth century.

The nation whose history is a series of heroic

conflicts and victories for popular freedom, whose
rule is an embodiment of equity in the remotest
corner of our most distant dependencies, most
alien also in race and creed, is surely in its
proper place when it undertakes to act as the
prime mover in the redress of the terrible
wrongs of the Christian subjects of the Ottoman Empire.

England has taken this prominent position—a
position so prominent that on her, above all others,
must rest the blame, if blame there be, for the
haunting horrors of Turkish misrule.

The Crimean War, with the Treaty of Paris,
the Treaty of Berlin, the Cyprus Convention, are
all witnesses of our manifold pledges. On this
point we have already said enough in these pages.
We, as a nation, have undertaken the task of
Turkish reforms, and we have ignominiously
failed. We have not only failed to redeem our
pledges, we have, by incessant ineffective admo-
nitions and corrosives directed to the sensitive
parts of the Sultan's nature, produced fresh irri-
tation, and induced new ordeals of persecution
for the wretched Armenians.

Lord Salisbury has, it is true, begun to exchange
not merely the language of bravado, but the bluff
speech of an English statesman—which was not
the least of his graces and claims to respect—for
a style of watery compliment which must help to
cheer the Sultan in his dreary solitude, and must
somewhat surprise the novice in politics who has

been so boldly checkmating his lordship ¯in St. ´
Petersburg.

Yielding to the blind impulses of the Jingoism
of the day, Lord Salisbury undertook, in 1878,
responsibilities which could not easily be discharged, and did so in a manner so provocative of
the jealousy of the Powers that they have never
forgiven him, and have ever since, quietly but
effectively, frustrated every feeble effort he has
made to introduce the Turkish reforms.

Lord Salisbury's, it must be remembered, was
the hand that tore up the provisions of the Treaty
of San Stefano guaranteeing deliverance to the
Armenians. His was the hand which drew up
the now dishonoured pledge of the Treaty of
Berlin, as well as the terms of the Cyprus Convention, by which the English nation was degraded into an ally and accomplice of the Turk in
his shameful misgovernment and oppression of
his Christian subjects.

These are now the chief honours which his
lordship has inherited from the historical transac-
tions of 1878, and which promise to give him
a unique name among the statesmen of England.

The case, then, both as regards the Powers of
Europe and England, stands thus :

The Sultan has pledged himself, by the most
solemn engagements, to remove all disabilities
from his subjects, and to seek their comfort and
happiness without distinction of race or religion.
The Powers are, at the same time, aware that, so

far from an effort being made to carry out these repeated engagements, the daily lot of his victims has been becoming more intolerable. The most overwhelming evidence has been laid before them from all sides that outrages surpassing anything almost, if not altogether, within the range of history have been planned and carried out by the Turkish Government. All the subterfuges of perjured officials of Ottoman misrule, and of others interested in concealing or minimizing the enormities, have utterly failed of their object. Not only do the common obligations of humanity press upon the signatories, but also their legal responsibilities, and most of all those of this country, however loudly disavowed. On this subject, in his eloquent protest against such a disavowal, and as emphasizing this responsibility, the Duke of Argyll says : ' It is not too much to say that England has twice saved Turkey from complete subjection since 1853. It is largely, mainly due to our action that she now exists at all as an independent Power. On both occasions we dragged the Powers of Europe along with us in maintaining the Ottoman Government. . . . The rest of Europe does share with us in the terrible responsibility of bolstering up a decaying empire *from sheer jealousy of each other as to the division of the spoils.* But we share it in an especial degree because our jealousy of Russia was, and still is, pre-eminent among all the other jealousies concerned.'

It may not be that, as Lord Derby cynically expressed it, 'the last word of the Eastern Question is, Who is to have Constantinople?' There can, however, be no doubt, on such an authority as we have just quoted, that the difficulty of the division of the spoils is the main obstacle to a prompt and satisfactory solution of the problem.

It cannot fail to have a demoralizing effect upon the nations of Europe to stand aloof and remain passive in the face of wrongs which they are pledged not only to redress, but to have prevented.

We have been hearing much of the danger of pressing too far for the fulfilment of these pledges of reform so profusely given by the Sultan. But is it, then, safe for England to let it be understood that she can be bullied out of her definite treaty engagements? When this discovery is once made, are we not likely to have our hands full enough of similar business?

The question is not closed. The credit of England, her influence among the Powers of Europe, demand a different ending.

No doubt the practical question is, What is now to be done? So far this is a question which concerns every nation in Europe, this country above all others, and every one in it capable of thinking on the subject. Our country has thrown its ægis over the Armenians, and entered into a solemn league and covenant for their protection, and we are bound to see that, in some fitting manner, that grand national trust shall be fulfilled. We have, as a self-governing people, an individual responsibility as to what a Parliament, elected by our suffrages, may or may not do with pledges tendered in our name. Surely our responsibilities, as a nation, are not discharged by permitting our ambassador at Constantinople, or our responsible ministers at Westminster, to give as they may see fit friendly, well-meaning advice to the Sultan.

Nor, again, can we hold that we, as a nation, atone for our betrayal of interests, dearer than life itself to the Armenians, by scanty doles of charitable relief to those whose distress we ought by every obligation of honour to have prevented. It is our bounden duty to give, and to give liberally, what financial relief we can afford. There is no true friend of the persecuted, homeless, starving Christians in Armenia who will not do their best to respond to the earnest appeals of the committee of the Armenian Relief Fund for some measure of help to these houseless, half-naked wanderers in woods and mountains, living in caves and hollow trees, and striving to support existence on greens and the leaves of the trees. It is something that our English nation is responding to these appeals. But the assistance is avowedly inadequate, so that only a small remnant of the sufferers can be relieved. Even were it otherwise, the horrible ordeal of butchery and foul lust goes on before the eyes

of Europe and the world. A letter from
Constantinople, May 30, 1896, says : ' The
Government measures are a perfect farce! We
have a terrible and new appeal this week, and
that is, for relief to the numbers of Armenian
maidens, who, having been taken by the Kurds
and Turks, and kept by them for several months,
are now returned to their villages in the pangs of
a prospective horrible motherhood. Who will
keep these unfortunates and their offspring? I
often ask myself, Is it not better to let these
miserable creatures die at once than continue a
wretched existence through the summer only to
die from starvation and cold next winter ?'

One other point remains to be emphasized—the
perpetrators of the massacre must be punished.

After the Lebanon massacres of 1860, France
and England saw the necessity of reading the
Sultan and his subjects a lesson that the two
Powers would not tolerate such outrage on the
Christian subjects of Turkey. The punishment of
the most deeply involved Pasha was demanded.
He was reluctantly put on trial, but acquitted,
Fuad Pasha, the Turkish Commissioner, declaring
that the punishment of a Pasha would greatly
excite the Mahommedan population. He was
promptly informed that the populace had better
keep their feelings well in hand, as he would be
held responsible for any disturbances, and in the
·event of such taking place, English and French
marines would occupy Damascus. The Turkish

13

Commissioner saw the game was up. The guilty Pasha was hanged forthwith, and there was no disturbance.

So long as it is understood that the Christian can be outraged with impunity, the plundering and murdering will continue. Till the punishment of the criminals has been sternly carried out no Christian life is worth a day's purchase. A premium is put on the outrages if it be supposed no punishment will fall on the offenders.

As regards the best practical solution of the problem, this may be safely left to the Government when once it has resolved to act. There is the scheme set forth and ably advocated by Canon MacColl in his pamphlet on ' England's Responsibility to Armenia,' and which follows the successful precedent of Lebanon. ' A constitution,' he says, ' must be drawn up for Armenia by some one acting on behalf of the great Powers, or those of them who have already intervened in this matter. And that constitution must insist as a minimum on the appointment of a Christian governor of Armenia, provided with some sort of force to maintain order : the governor either to be appointed directly by the Powers or subject to their approval, and irremovable without their sanction.' All the objections to this scheme were brought against the similar scheme of Lebanon, and were found to be utterly baseless. The Powers assumed an attitude of firmness, and the Lebanon experiment triumphed.

Ere we leave this subject, we may mention the scheme which Mr. Greene refers to as one of the most likely, having also the approval of Professor Bryce and the Phil-Armenian Society. This method is that of 'radical and vigorous administrative reforms, which the European Powers should initiate and report to Turkey, instead of *vice versâ*, as arranged in Article LXI. of the Berlin Treaty.'

But our task is now done. We have glanced at the drama of Armenian life both in earlier and later times. We have seen a native dynasty, or, rather, series of dynasties, come and go. We have watched the dawn of a new light on the hills and valleys of the country of Ararat, as they are trodden by the feet of the apostolic St. Gregory, and Armenia takes its place of honour among the nations as the first to give its glad welcome to the message of the Gospel. Around this sacred national shrine, it has been seen, all that is truly noble and enduring in the life of this people has henceforth revolved. Around it lie scattered, in profuse abundance, the martyred ashes of many generations of worshippers.

Our survey has led us to consider some outstanding points in the ascending arc of the rise and progress of the Turkish Empire. The influence of Islam has been noted, as it has influenced the character and rule of the Turk, and shaped and coloured the destiny of the Armenians.

We have further traced, so far, the course of

decline. We have indicated the vast programme
and some steps in the formidable advances of
Russia towards the acme of her ambition. The
motto of that movement has ever been, and still
is, the same—' Nulla vestigia retrorsum.'

We have stood by the sick-bed of the dying
barbarian despot, and beheld his strange tenacity
of existence, his prostrations, and wonderful re-
coveries.

We have witnessed the spectacle of the Concert
of Europe combining and agreeing on almost
nothing else save in an attempt to maintain the
ghastly moribund tyrant on his tottering throne.

As we linger over this region of stirring associations, ancient and modern, we see in and around
the fatherland of the children of Haik, and in the
remotest regions of their dispersion through Asia
Minor, one far-reaching Aceldama.

We tread the solitudes of a vast necropolis.
Around us lie the mangled corpses of men, women,
and children, who, ere they were thrust, many of
them still alive, into the graves they had been
compelled to dig for themselves, had endured every
agony of mind and body which it is possible for
human beings to undergo. Their long-protracted
dying agonies had been the sport of the miscreants
who meantime boasted that they were carrying
out the express orders of the Sultan.

The burying-ground of these massacred, martyred Armenians is lined all around by a fast thin-
ning circle of mourners, whose own doom is visibly

impending, and whose sobs and wails are a ceaseless funeral dirge falling on 'the dull, cold ear of
death,' but falling also on the not less apathetic
ear of their living and pledged protectors. Among
these cold insensate spectators we behold the
Powers of Christian Europe, and foremost among
them Christian England, as represented by the
present Premier. Here is the picture of a single
corner of these saddest of all the realms of
death.

'What I myself saw,' says an eye-witness, 'this
Friday afternoon is for ever engraven on my mind
as the most horrible sight a man can see. I went
with one of the cavasses of the English Legation,
a soldier my interpreter, and a photographer
(Armenian) to the Armenian Gregorian Cemetery.
The municipality had sent down a number of
bodies, friends had brought more, and a horrible
sight met my eyes. Along the wall on the north,
in a row twenty feet wide and a hundred and fifty
feet long, lay three hundred and twenty-one dead
bodies of the massacred Armenians. Many were
fearfully mangled and mutilated. I saw one with
his face completely smashed in with a blow of
some heavy weapon after he was killed. I saw
some with their necks almost severed by a sword-
cut. One I saw whose whole chest had been
skinned, his fore-arms had been cut off, while
the upper arm was skinned of flesh. I asked if
the dogs had done this. " No, the Turks did it
with their knives." A dozen bodies were half

burned. All the corpses had been rifled of all
their clothes except a cotton under-garment or
two. These white under-clothes were stained
with the blood of the dead, presenting a fearful
sight. The faces of many were disfigured beyond
recognition, and all had been thrown down, face
foremost, in the dust of the streets and the mud of
the gutters, so that all were black with clotted
blood and dust. Some were stark naked, and
everybody seemed to have at least two wounds,
and some a dozen. In this list of dead there were
only three women, two babies, a number of young
children, and about thirty young boys of fifteen to
twenty.

'A crowd of a thousand people, mostly Armenians, watched me taking photographs of their
dead. Many were weeping beside their dead
fathers or husbands. The Armenian photographer
saw two children, relatives of his, among the dead.
Some Armenian workmen were engaged excavating
a deep trench twenty feet square close by, to bury
the corpses. Here, too, was a peculiar scene.
The space of this trench contained many graves,
and on one side were a number of skulls, perhaps twenty in all, and a pile of bones found
in the excavating. I left the sad sight sick at
heart.'

Will none of these mournful sights and sounds
move, in any degree, the heart and conscience of
the British nation, and constrain us to prompt
and vigorous action ? Alas! for many thousands

of Armenians now sleeping their last sleep in
those rude trenches, for many thousands more
wearing out a few days of hopeless degradation,
there is no effective service we can now render!
The opportunity has been for ever lost.

Yet still, ere the brutal Turk make a full end,
is there no sympathy in Christian hearts, in the
heart of Great Britain, no dread of the inevitable
retribution, to constrain us to call, as with the
blast of a trumpet, for a prompt and final arrest
on these orgies of death and dishonour worse
than death? There is assuredly no time to lose.
It is now or never that authoritative summons
must sound forth.

Abdul Hamid still sits secure in the recesses
of the Yildiz Kiosk — free to organize fresh
massacres. Not one of the perpetrators of the
outrages on the Armenians has been punished
for his crimes. The more prominent of them
have been decorated in token of imperial favour.

Yet the solemn farce of Commissions of Inquiry
goes on, and our Government is content to
simulate approval of the action which His
Majesty has been good enough to take.

Apart from all consideration of the claims and
interests of the Armenians, our own vaunted
British interests, our prestige in the East demand
that it should not be understood that the Sultan
has escaped the penalty of his long arrears of
flagrant crimes, and of his studied insults to this
country. An attitude of complicity with the

foulest crimes which have disgraced the history of the world has been and is being forced upon the British nation. Are we for ever to stand idly by and see, without one generous impulse, the still protracted agony of the Christians we have pledged our honour to protect ? Has not the time arrived for England to show that she feels acutely that she has been acting out of character, and must now resume her proper *rôle*, which is not that of the smiling friend and ally of the blood-stained tyrant, but the liberator of his miserable victim ?

Is true freedom but to break
Fetters for our own dear sake.
And, with leathern hearts, forget
That we owe mankind a debt ?
No ! true freedom is to share
All the chains our brothers wear,
And, with heart and hand, to be
Earnest to make others free !

THE END.

Elliot Stock, Paternoster Row, London.

In crown 8vo, cloth, price 5s.

HISTORICAL SKETCH
OF ARMENIA

AND THE ARMENIANS, IN ANCIENT AND MODERN TIMES.

BY AN OLD INDIAN:

Rev W. STEPHEN, Kelty, Blairadam, *Author of "Life and Writings of Michael Bruce."*

OPINIONS OF THE PRESS.

" A well-constructed and excellently written survey of the past and of the most salient points of the present of Armenia."—*Spectator.*

" While nothing of importance has been omitted, nothing irrelevant has been included, and the result is an excellent little work which ought to find many thousands of readers at the present crisis. . . . We commend the study of the Russo-Turkish relations as contained in this little volume to those who desire a key to the history of the Eastern Question during the last half-century,"—*Daily Chronicle.*

" Written with peculiar knowledge, and will be read with advantage by everyone who is interested in the subject."—*Scotsman.*

" It would be surprising if this volume should not become a popular hand-book on the Armenian aspect of the Eastern Question."—*Dundee Advertiser.*

" We have pleasure in recommending this volume to public notice as the most concise and convincing testimony we have yet seen on this momentous question. Our readers who want knowledge on this subject will get all they require from this excellent little volume."—*Perthshire Advertiser.*

" The story of Ancient Armenia is a deeply interesting one, and the Old Indian tells it with much vigour and animation, and with full knowledge of the subject, the result, evidently, of a great deal of research."—*Aberdeen Journal.*

" Deals thoroughly with the whole Eastern Question."—*Christian World.*

" The best hand-book on the subject that has yet appeared."—
Kinross-shire Advertiser.

* 9 7 8 3 3 3 7 2 8 8 2 8 0 *